WHY THEY FOLLOW

WHY THEY FOLLOW

Lessons in Church Communication
from That One Lost Sheep

MATTHEW WARNER

Published by Word on Fire, Elk Grove Village, IL 60007
© 2023 by Matthew Warner
Printed in the United States of America
All rights reserved

Cover design, typesetting, and interior art direction
by Rozann Lee and Cassie Bielak

First printing, July 2023

ISBN: 978-1-68578-040-1

Library of Congress Control Number: 2022912396

"Go after the one that is lost . . ."

—Luke 15:4

Contents

Foreword by Uno the Sheep   ix

PART I: GUIDING PRINCIPLES

1. Nobody Was There	3
2. Here's Why They Follow	13
3. The Message They Hear	19
4. What's at Stake?	25
5. Context Matters	38
6. Why Should They Trust You?	49
7. Cultivating Soil	59
8. Navigating the Digital Landscape	64

PART II: PRACTICAL LESSONS

9. How to Add Followers	79
10. Don't Assume They Know	92
11. How to Get Their Attention	100

12. Say Different Things to Different People   109

13. Did You Miss Me?   117

14. The Best Communication Channels   122

15. Say Less, Communicate More   130

16. Are You Listening?   138

17. Doing It on Purpose   145

18. Invitations That Work   158

19. The #1 Reason People Open
Your Email (or Anything)   163

20. Asking for Money   169

21. Don't Say It; Do It   183

22. Hangups, Hurdles, and Help   192

23. My Hope   205

What's Next?   208

Acknowledgments   211

Notes   212

Foreword

Uno the Sheep

You may not realize it yet, but you already know me. My name is Uno. I'm that one lost sheep from the Gospels. You know . . . the one the shepherd leaves the ninety-nine to go after? Hi.

I'm all around you, in the poor and the lonely. In the unloved and the hopeless. In our homes and pews. In everyone we meet, including in that lovely face you see in the mirror.

For over a decade now I've been working with Flocknote to help over ten thousand churches communicate with and lead their flocks (of all sheeps and sizes). In that time, we've learned a lot of lessons—what works, what doesn't, and the most common reasons churches are struggling to engage their people today.

Matthew Warner put the most important lessons we've learned along the way into this little book for you and your church to learn from. I helped. Well, I mostly just sheered him on. I promise he doesn't make as many sheep puns as I do (he's not as funny as me, bless him).

On behalf of the Flocknote team, I want to say thank you for the important work you do. Rest assured, we pray for you daily. I hope the lessons that follow will inspire you, challenge you, and greatly benefit your ministry as you go after those lost sheep, make disciples, and change the world.

> *"Which one of you, having a hundred sheep*
> *and losing one of them, does not leave the*
> *ninety-nine in the wilderness and go after*
> *the one that is lost until he finds it?"*
> —Luke 15:4

PART I

GUIDING PRINCIPLES

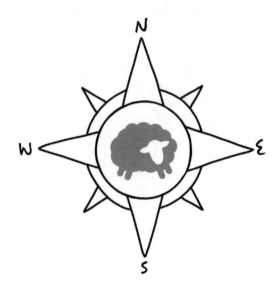

CHAPTER ONE

Nobody Was There

Nobody was there. I was in shock. Here he was in the flesh—one of my heroes, a best-selling author and one of the most brilliant writers and thinkers of our time—speaking at my parish. Having had my life changed by dozens of his books, I was exceptionally eager to snag a good seat and hear what he had to say. Well, finding a seat wasn't the problem.

The church should have been standing room only, but instead I saw maybe thirty-five folks scattered amongst mostly empty pews. I knew there were thousands of people within ten miles who would have loved to be there. Where was everybody? Why weren't they there?

I quickly realized the reason nobody was there: Nobody knew about it. Because nobody had told them about it. It really was that simple. Our leaders simply didn't have an effective way to get important and timely information directly to most of the flock.

The spark from that moment lit a fire in my life that still burns to this day.

WHAT'S KEEPING YOU IN THE CHURCH?

Not long before that moment, I was on a snowboarding trip and sitting at the end of a long dinner table at a noisy restaurant. Seated at the opposite end of the table was a slightly older friend who everyone admired, though our worldviews were quite different. That evening, he asked me a question I will never forget and that changed my life forever. Very loudly in front of five to six other friends he asked, "Hey Matt, what's keeping you in the Church?"

I actually don't remember how I answered, but I do remember how I felt: stupid. Nobody had asked me that question so directly before, and I was embarrassed that I wasn't ready with a good answer. So I went looking for one. I started asking questions and digging for answers. What I found blew my mind. Because what I discovered was a Church filled with treasure upon treasure upon treasure. I couldn't believe it. The more questions I'd ask and the deeper I'd go, the more satisfying the answers became. I was in awe at what I found. From then on, I was all in.

In stark contrast, and at the exact same time, so many of my peers were getting asked this same question (sometimes explicitly, but most often implicitly, by the world): What's keeping you in the Church? Yet their response was very different. They were getting less and less committed to their faith, finding it irrelevant, outdated, uninteresting, or outright incompatible with the life they wanted to live. When I would speak to them about why they were drifting away, it became immediately clear that they had no idea what they were leaving.

4

Where I saw the greatest treasures of humankind, they saw yesterday's news. How could we each be seeing the same thing so differently? How can the same message sound so different to different people?

SIGNS OF THE TIMES

Consider this graph showing the percentage of Americans calling themselves Christian:

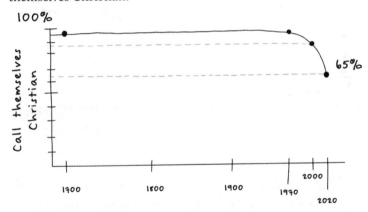

For most of our country's history, well over 90% of our people called themselves Christian. In 1970, it was still around 90%, having held very steady for centuries. But by 2000, only thirty years later, it had suddenly dropped to 80%, a dramatic shift from the previous few hundred years. Today, only twenty more years later, it's down still dramatically further to 65%. Not only are Americans rapidly becoming less Christian, but we are doing so at an increasing rate. This is happening across all demographics and denominations, but especially among young people.

Consider it from the angle of those who now claim "no religion."

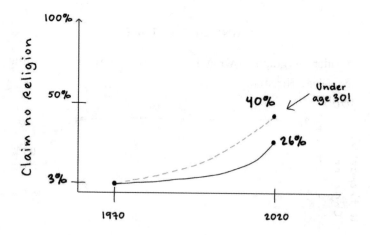

Fifty years ago, only 3% of people claimed no religious affiliation. Today, the number is 26% (more than eight times larger). Far more troubling, for those under age thirty, a whopping 40% claim no religious affiliation. Even more sobering, these graphs are really only showing the lagging indicators of more meaningful metrics, like actual Sunday church attendance or whether people are authentically living Christian lives, which all measure worse still.

But we are not going to spend this book diving into depressing statistics that only confirm what you already know. Instead, I'm going to give you some key insights that will help turn things around.

IT'S A COMMUNICATION PROBLEM

We are half-hearted creatures, fooling about with drink
and sex and ambition when infinite joy is offered us,
like an ignorant child who wants to go on making
mud pies in a slum because he cannot imagine
what is meant by the offer of a holiday at
the sea. We are far too easily pleased.
—C.S. Lewis

Christianity offers infinite joy and the only way to overcome death. It is a smart religion, with tremendous intellectual and spiritual richness and depth. It offers helpful and genius insights into every aspect of life, both personal and societal. It is literally the greatest treasure fathomable. But the world increasingly rejects it anyway. Why do people continue to drift away in record numbers? Why don't they know what they're leaving? Because it hasn't been communicated to them. Our message, quite simply, has not gotten through.

It's not enough to simply possess valuable treasure and smart ideas. We must also be able to communicate what we have to others in smart ways. And we must learn to do so amidst a noisy and quickly evolving media landscape that is increasingly working against us. At the core of the Christian mission is the need to communicate.

THE SACRED WORK

Communication is not one task among many, nor only the work of one department or person. It is an essential skill for every leader. And it is sacred work.

The definition of *communicate* is to give, to impart, or to transmit something in order that you might share it in common. Its Latin root (*communicare*) means to make common, to share, or to join with. The very purpose of communication is to bring about communion. The strength of every community is built upon successful communication—the sharing of something in common. Our church communities are crumbling because the common bonds that we share have grown weaker and are losing out to other, stronger cultural forces.

All genuine communication of truth is sacred, since it leads to the sharing in common of Truth himself (Jesus), a community we call the Church. But remember, communication is not simply proclaiming things. To have communicated something is to have it successfully received by the person on the other end (i.e., to share it in common). Too often we say a lot but communicate little. And without successful communication you have no community, no communion, no Church, no Body of Christ.

This is the sacred work of every leader in the Church and the means by which we seek to fulfill Jesus' prayer that we may all be one (John 17:21). To communicate is sacred work, and it is your work.

QUITTING

Soon after those life-changing experiences, I quit my job as a computer engineer and went on a mission to build a more connected Church—a Church that knows how to communicate and share its treasures. I wanted to make sure everyone knew the answer to the question "What's keeping you in the Church?" There were many years of hard lessons to be learned and tough sacrifices to be made, and I had the challenge of sorting through the vast array of ever-evolving communication techniques and technologies to figure out what really works. But our team persisted and built Flocknote, an award-winning, employee-owned software company with record growth and a community of 200,000+ church leaders and over 10,000 churches.

Another lesson I learned, however, is that tools will only take you so far. Though Flocknote created an amazing software tool (for communication, member database management, online payments, and more), solving the deeper, more fundamental challenge—making sure our message successfully makes it through—takes more than just having the right tools. It takes leaders who know how to use them. It takes great communicators.

Over these many years, I've seen thousands of churches succeed and many others flounder. I've personally spent twenty years on various pastoral councils, leading ministries at my own church, traveling all over the country speaking to thousands of church leaders, leading conferences, podcasting, blogging, writing books, and creating innovative media projects that have reached hundreds of thousands of people—all while getting to lead a successful, fast-growing team of mission-driven people here at Flocknote. I've seen both what works and what common mistakes hold churches back.

The good news? Most all of it can be fixed.

GET READY

No matter which department you work in, how high (or low) you are on the totem pole, how tech-savvy you are, or how long you've been at it, I believe you and your team will find something in this book that will help you grow as leaders and communicators. The first major part of this book focuses on the big foundational ideas that successful communicators and leaders should understand. If we get these foundational parts right, the rest is easy. If we get these wrong, the rest doesn't matter. I believe the main reasons people today are leaving the faith in record numbers—while having no idea what treasures they are leaving behind—have more to do with the foundational issues in part I of this book than the practical lessons found in part II. So even though you may already be familiar with some of the key ideas in part I, it is worth revisiting them to assess how well your team is doing. Once you address those, all the lessons in the second part of the book become much more relevant and powerful.

You are doing inspiring, important, and sacred work. You should know that everything in this book I learned from many years of observing, working with, and listening to leaders just like you. It is a privilege to share it all with you here, and I pray it is a blessing to you and your ministry.

READING TIPS

- Grab your highlighter or favorite writing utensil. Mark this book up as you read, dog-ear pages, and take notes!

- Consider getting ten copies of the book and giving one to each of your staff and other ministry leaders.

- Ask each person to read it (which only takes a few hours), take notes, and come prepared to your next team meeting ready to discuss. Before you begin, quickly answer the following questions (don't overthink them, just whatever immediately comes to mind):
  - ▸ What's keeping you in the Church?
  - ▸ What are your big goals this year as a church or ministry?

CHAPTER TWO

Here's Why They Follow

What makes somebody a leader? The answer is quite simple: they have followers. Not employees, or customers, or constituents, but followers. But how does someone get followers? Why do people follow anyone at all?

Here are four takes from four different perspectives: the Pragmatist, the CEO, the Researcher, and Jesus. Every church leader should know and understand all of these answers. Each provides helpful insights for our work and will help us unpack the lessons in this book.

THE PRAGMATIST

On its face, why somebody follows you as a leader is quite logical and practical. It can be broken down into two basic questions which undergird the whole of this book:

1. Do they want to go where you're going?

2. Do they believe that you can get them there?

If people aren't following where you're trying to lead them, then their answer to one of those two questions is likely no.

Do they want to go where you're going? If you're not sure, consider the following questions:

- Have you clearly communicated an inspiring vision they'd like to achieve?
- Do they like your plan and the role they get to play in it?
- Are they willing to pay the cost to go (i.e., make the necessary sacrifices)?
- Do they believe they are worthy, themselves, of going?
- Do they truly want to go where you're going?

Do they believe you can get them there? They may love your vision and desperately want to go there, but they still won't follow unless they also:

- Believe the goal is achievable in the first place.
- Believe that you, the leader, are capable of achieving this goal.
- Believe that you are interested in getting *them* there too (not just using them so that you can get there yourself).

Generally, if we can inspire a yes to these two fundamental questions, they will follow. The concept is simple. Of course, communicating all of that successfully is the hard part and the focus of this book.

THE CEO

The CEO perspective on *why people follow* is helpful for leading not only your core volunteers and staff but also any member of your flock. The best CEOs don't want a workforce of mercenaries, just working for a paycheck. They want an army of missionaries—passionate, committed, believers in the mission. But how do such leaders engage, motivate, and inspire a group of people to become that (i.e., turn them into true followers)?

Well, they start by realizing that you surely can't do it by simply paying people more and more money. That doesn't work. In fact, once somebody has enough pay for their work (their basic needs and some wants are met), there are three other things that people value even more than money and that have the potential to transform them into true followers: (1) meaningful work, (2) personal growth, and (3) responsibility.

The beautiful thing about each of these is that what your church is doing has the potential to satisfy each of these beyond anything else in this world. Living the Christian life is the epitome of every one of these things—the most meaningful work, genius insight into how to live, and the realization that each of us is needed to achieve the mission. The trouble is that our flock doesn't always make that connection themselves. We have to help them.

THE RESEARCHER

Gallup (the well-respected polling and research group) asked ten thousand people what they want from the leaders they choose to follow. The answers basically boiled down to these four things:

1. Hope
2. Trust
3. Compassion
4. Stability

On first look, these answers probably aren't surprising. They're almost boring. I think what may surprise people more is what's not on the list. People aren't primarily looking for charismatic, exciting, innovative, dynamic leaders, though that's often what we picture when we think of a great leader. These other four things—hope, trust, compassion, and stability—are far more important features. The good news is that every leader can learn to cultivate and convey them.

JESUS

Finally, and most importantly, we come to what Jesus says on this topic. In the Gospel of John, Jesus gives us a most profound insight as to why people follow while also indirectly summing up all of these other perspectives:

> Very truly, I tell you, anyone who does not enter the sheepfold by the gate but climbs in by another way is a thief and a bandit. The one who enters by the gate is the shepherd of the sheep. The gatekeeper opens the gate for him, and the sheep hear his voice. He calls his own sheep by name and leads them out. When he has brought out all his own, he goes ahead of them, and *the sheep follow him because they know his voice.* They will not follow a stranger, but they will run from him because they do not know the voice of strangers. (John 10:1–5; emphasis added)

Let's break that down. A good shepherd:

- Enters by the gate (doesn't take shortcuts in the relationship),
- Calls them by name,
- Retrieves each individual sheep,
- Then leads them and they follow. Why? Because they know his voice.

Each of these four perspectives will be helpful as we unpack the lessons in this book. As you can see, God set us up for success. What humans desire most can all be found most perfectly in him, through his Bride the Church. As leaders, it is our job to figure out how to communicate it. That is the task of the rest of this book.

REFLECT

- What are you leading your flock to do or accomplish right now? Is it meaningful to them? (I.e., do they want to go where you are going?)

- What are some ways that you currently offer meaningful work? (For your staff and volunteers? For every member of your community?)

- How well do they know your voice? (Do you call them by name?)

CHAPTER THREE

The Message They Hear

"Wah wah woh wah wah . . . wah woh wah."
—Charlie Brown's teacher

That's us. Charlie Brown's teacher. We think we're explaining ourselves with perfect clarity, but a lot of people today aren't hearing it the same way we are. To fix this, we need to understand the many factors that go into creating any message and determining whether it's successfully received on the other side. That begins with recognizing that the message received on the other end is not simply "what I say."

$$\text{The message} \neq \text{"what I say"}$$

The equation is much more complicated—impossibly complicated really. Something more like this, for example:

$$\text{The message} = \left(\frac{\text{"what I say"} \times \text{form} \times \text{delivery} + \text{my example}}{\text{recipient bias} + \text{baggage}} \right)^{\text{recipient needs}}$$
$$\times \left(\text{worldview} + \text{context} \right) \times \text{pi} \times \left(\begin{array}{c} \text{My relationship} \\ \text{with them} \end{array} \right)$$

(You're probably wondering why pi is part of the equation. Well, that's because one of the greatest mathematical constants of the universe is that food, especially pizza pie, plays a huge role in getting people to pay attention and therefore getting the message through. Never underestimate the power of sharing a meal together.)

Now, the point here is not to overanalyze my made-up equation. The takeaway is that many, many things all come together in complex ways to ultimately form the message that comes out the other side.

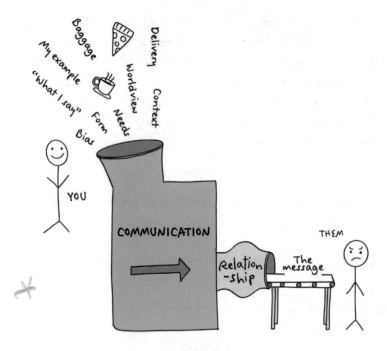

There is so much more to the equation than simply what we say (which is also important). All these other variables are critical to focus on to communicate successfully (all of which we'll be exploring throughout the book). Ignore any of them and you may be saying the most beautiful things but still communicating nothing (or something entirely different than you intend).

If math and machines are not your thing, then perhaps a funny text message will help make a similar point:

When it comes to communicating and making sure the right message comes out the other side, context matters. History matters. Who you are matters. Relationship matters. In fact, of all these many factors, *relationship is the most important transmission line when it comes to spreading the faith.*

One might assume that surely today we are all more connected than ever. But it's not true. We may be more connected by wires and bits than ever before. We may be more connected to information than ever before. But our human relationships (the connections that matter most, particularly for evangelization and transmission of the faith) may perhaps be at all-time lows. We have more broken families, more depression and loneliness, transient homes, shallower roots, less connection with neighbors, fewer close friends, and a cultural obsession with individualism and self-expression (instead of an emphasis on others and relationships).

We can spend all kinds of time working on the words to say it, the content to convey it, or the equipment to transmit it. But what is really needed most urgently today is the messy, demanding work of creating, building, and nourishing the strong, stable, healthy individual relationships required to carry the message in the first place. A weak relationship means a weak signal comes out the other end. A great relationship, on the other hand, is a highway to being heard.

WHO YOU ARE

When God wanted to communicate to us his most important word, he used flesh ("the Word became flesh," as we read in John 1). He didn't just tell us who he is; he embodied it. Similarly, we must also become (embody) what we want to say. Evangelization is proclaiming the Good News not primarily by sharing *information* (what you say) but rather by sharing your friendship with Jesus (who you are). That means we must first have such a friendship to share, a deeply personal relationship with the risen Lord, cultivated through prayer and authentic Christian living. A relationship that has so obviously transformed your life and showed you the world in a new, refreshing, life-changing way. Only then can you carry and transmit the message without extinguishing it in the process.

When somebody encounters a message like that, a person in such a friendship with Jesus, it cannot be easily shrugged off or ignored, as they do to so much of what we say. On the contrary, such an encounter always changes you. That's evangelization. It wakes people up and turns their worlds upside down.

That's how God communicates. And God's favorite medium to communicate that with is you.

WHAT PEOPLE FOLLOW

In the end, people aren't going to follow your message, your ideas, or your organization. They are going to follow you. All of these lessons about leadership and communication are useless without a human person like you to bring them to life, recruiting others and charging forward into action.

It's the same with "vision." A vision does not exist apart from the person who "sees" it. It only becomes a vision once a leader like you uses your imagination to "see" it into existence—to see something that does not exist yet but perhaps one day could. And the only way others can come to see that same vision and follow you there is if you are able to communicate that vision to them.

We need you. Your church needs you. Somebody out there, right now, needs you to build a relationship with them and to share your friendship with Jesus. We need you to communicate a meaningful vision of a future that people are motivated to bring to life, and we need you to lead us there.

REFLECT

- When it comes to communicating your "message," have you been considering the entire equation (beyond just what you say)? What are some areas you feel you should focus on more?

- Are there people you're having trouble engaging with or breaking through to? Begin by examining your relationship with them. What can you do to build a stronger relationship with them first?

CHAPTER FOUR

What's at Stake?

"Fight and you may die.
Run, and you'll live . . . at least a while."
—William Wallace, *Braveheart*

William Wallace, the famed Scottish warrior, got almost everything wrong going into the Battle of Stirling Bridge to try and win Scottish independence. Not enough men. Bad politics. Inferior weapons. He was trying to lead a bunch of divided clans against far superior forces.

So why did this ragtag rabble of disorganized factions and farmers follow William Wallace into a risky battle? It wasn't because he convinced them they were going to win or that their lives would be spared. It's because he was able to clearly communicate what was actually at stake. In his speech to convince the men to stay and fight (in the movie), he goes on to cry out, "They may take our lives, but they'll never take our freedommmmm!"

In that moment, he makes clear that the choice is not "Do I risk my life today or not?" No. The real choice in that moment was either to remain free (fight) or to surrender their freedom (run away). Once he makes that clear—even though the cost remains high—the right choice becomes obvious.

You may feel like William Wallace at your church. High stakes. Underfunded. Tired. Jaded. Not enough volunteers. Division. Frustrating technology. Internal drama. But fear not. The Apostles were there too. All they had was the Gospel and the Holy Spirit. Nothing but spiritual treasure (true freedom) in exchange for great cost (laying down your life). And that's all we need today, but it only works if, like William Wallace, we can communicate what is truly at stake.

GETTING THEM OFF THE COUCH

"Jesus was the only one that ever raised the dead, and he shouldn't have done it. He thrown everything off balance."

—The Misfit (via Flannery O'Connor)

Spiritual complacency, Flannery O'Connor suggests, is perhaps the greatest block to Christianity. It's very difficult to break through to and communicate with somebody who just doesn't seem to care. The modern attitude seems to be that everything in humans is basically in order—that all is well. If that's true, Jesus becomes merely a great spiritual teacher and no longer a Savior. And our churches become just nice groups of people to do life with rather than lifeboats.

And while it's a lovely thing to create a nice group of people to do life with, that's not the mission of the Church. There is something big at stake. C.S. Lewis wisely pointed out that "Christianity is a statement which, if false, is of no importance, and, if true, of infinite importance. The only thing it cannot be is moderately important." Unfortunately, at many churches it all feels a bit moderately important. They no longer act as if there is something big at stake. They may think they do, but that is not apparent when you walk in the doors or read their communications. This is a key reason so many people continue to disengage; it just doesn't feel like it matters all that much.

If I show up, nothing different happens. If I stop showing up, nobody missed me. If I give money or not, seems like everything is the same. If I commit or not, no difference. Nothing at stake. Not going anywhere. We shouldn't be surprised people are drifting away from something like that.

People today are actually highly engaged in the things they believe matter most. They passionately follow leaders who have communicated that something they care about is at stake:

"If the other party wins, America will be set back one hundred years."

"If you give us $20/month, a whole village will get clean water for a year."

"Grow your beard, help to end cancer."

"Buy now . . . before tickets sell out!"

"Don't miss the premiere tonight" (or you'll be left out of the conversation tomorrow).

When people know something they care about is at stake, they become highly motivated and engaged.

WHY?

Every group needs a big *why*—the big vision. It is the Something Worth Sacrificing Everything Else For. The Big Hairy Audacious Goal. It's the destination you are leading them toward. The reason the tribe exists. A meaningful mission. Putting a man on the moon (or Elon Musk's "Making humans a multi-planetary species"). Climbing Mt. Everest. Saving the world. Heaven together.

When leaders set out to do big things, people take notice. If those people want to go there too and believe you can get them there, then they make big sacrifices to help make it happen or die trying. This is ultimately what gives people hope (the belief that tomorrow can be better than today). The question is: What Big Thing are you leading people to do? If you want big commitments, big conversions, big participation, big checks, then communicate a big vision and set big goals. Do something big.

IN THE ABSENCE OF LARGE PURPOSE

The preaching is boring. The coffee is too strong. Somebody's sitting in my pew. The cantor is off-key. There isn't enough parking. The website looks outdated. The new carpet in the sanctuary . . . [eye roll].

This kind of complaining starts happening in the absence of large purpose. When people forget they are doing something big, then little things start to feel like big things and cause problems. If you want less complaining about the little things, hand them something Big to do. It's the same with little excuses.

I don't have time. There's no room in the budget. Maybe after we do [fill in the blank] first.

When your vision is small, small excuses derail it. When the goals you set and ask your people to support are small, their commitment is small. The other bigger things in their life will take precedence. Being "too busy," having "no room in the budget," or "not feeling like it" all become acceptable reasons to just keep doing the same thing (or nothing). If little excuses are derailing your efforts, perhaps the vision isn't big enough yet (or hasn't been clearly communicated).

This is also a reason why there is so much division in our world today. We emphasize and celebrate our many individual differences (and we should), but what is missing is an overarching unity of purpose that is still more important and that brings us together *despite those differences*. The strongest relationships are not face to face, but shoulder to shoulder, where two people together are focused on something that transcends them. This could be a common foe, a unified vision, an ideal, a shared love of something else. Without it, we obsess about our differences and become more divided. We see it in every area of society—marriage, politics, work, the Church. God made a wonderfully diverse and beautiful world. Our differences are part of what makes it so beautiful, but just being different or diverse is not a foundation for a meaningful life. The Body of Christ has many diverse parts, but each is meaningless without the Body itself, which unifies them all and gives them purpose. A hand, heart, or lung has no purpose without the body. Unity is more important.

This is what the Bible means in Proverbs 29:18 when it says, "Where there is no vision, the people perish" (KJV). The vision—this large purpose—is what unifies and holds a people together. Without it, the community will slowly disintegrate.

This absence of large purpose no doubt also contributes to the rise in all kinds of vice today. A man actively engaged in battle or saving the life of his family doesn't set down his sword to indulge in video games, binge-watch TV, view pornography, or get drunk. But when he feels like he is no longer needed or there is nothing left to fight for, those things are more likely to creep in. If you want your flock to stick together, go to battle together. Stand for something. Tackle something big together. Set your sights on something large and meaningful and heartbreakingly beautiful and march shoulder to shoulder toward it.

BRING YOUR MISSION STATEMENT TO LIFE

President John F. Kennedy didn't inspire a nation by saying, "Let's explore outer space more!" Or "I hope we can win the space race." He said, "We're going to put a man on the moon this decade." And that made all the difference! The way he formulated it was specific, concrete, and enchanting, and it gripped the imagination of the world. The goal was clear, exciting, and potentially achievable in the perceivable future (seven years later Neil Armstrong stepped foot on the lunar surface).

We need to do that with our own churches' mission statements: bring it to life with something bold and audacious that will grip the imagination of your flock and get them off the couch and into the game.

Things like:

- Fully fund a mission in another country (or across town).
- Get every married couple to a marriage retreat in the next three years.
- Make sure every lonely person in our county (shut-ins, elderly, assisted living centers) gets a visit every month.
- Create the #1 food pantry in the state.
- Get every high schooler to a retreat before leaving for college.
- Develop a national award–winning choir.

- Triple the size of our small group participation.
- Get every family to do a Bible study together this year.
- Personally invite every family in our town to something at our church.
- Start a school whose #1 goal is cultivating virtue and making saints.
- Build a church so magnificent that our great, great grandchildren are astonished at how much we must have loved God—a space that reorients every person's heart more toward God and the transcendent every time they walk through its doors.

The options are endless. But find something that brings your mission statement to life in a challenging, inspiring way. Be specific so people know if and when you've achieved it and can visualize what success looks like. Clearly communicate both (1) what the fruits will be and (2) what weighs in the balance (i.e., what happens if you don't achieve it). That's what it means to communicate *what is at stake*—what will be won or lost depending on if we achieve this goal? It is the tension between those two things that propels people to participate.

Here's a simple example to illustrate the point:

Problem	Our children are going away to college and losing their faith.
Goal	Provide an education (new type of school) that helps them fall in love with living the faith.
What's at stake?	You can either (a) donate $X each to start this school and save the souls of some children, or (b) don't do that and let them continue to abandon their faith in record numbers.

In other words, how much does it matter if you succeed? If you're starting a school because it's a nice thing to do or because it'd be nice for families to have a school ten minutes closer, there simply isn't much at stake. That's not the kind of thing that inspires people to sacrifice their Saturdays and salaries. But if you can clearly communicate that something big weighs in the balance—as often does in your ministry—magic starts to happen. Be bold. Create tension. Give them a clear choice that compels them into meaningful action.

WHAT IT COSTS

What people don't realize is how much religion costs.
They think faith is a big electric blanket,
when of course it is the cross.

—Flannery O'Connor

It's tempting to shy away from the demands of the faith in hopes of making it more attractive. This is a mistake.

First, people know there is *no such thing as a free lunch*. Whenever they are offered something that is free or too good to be true, they know there is a catch. There always is. If we invite them to an epic story but it doesn't cost them anything, they know it's a joke, a ruse, a lie. Epic stories always cost the characters something epic.

Second, people often value things based on what they cost. If something costs little, it's probably worth little. If it costs a lot, it's probably worth a lot. If we define Christianity as T.S. Eliot did, as "a condition of complete simplicity (costing not less than everything)," that helps communicate the true value of what is being offered (eternal life).

Third, people want to be challenged to reach their potential—they want to find out what they are made of. They want somebody to accept them but also expect more of them (what they are capable of . . . which is incredible!). They want to live and not waste this life. Deep down we know we were made for perfect love, which means giving ourselves fully to something other than ourselves. So as we survey the many philosophies of the world, we subconsciously know that the true one will demand everything (and be worth everything).

Jesus asks for everything. If we are not lovingly communicating these extreme demands of the faith, we are not only miscommunicating the faith but hiding one of its most attractive dimensions! The easier we make it sound, the less we expect of people, the less it costs, the less at stake . . . the more bored they get. Our whole value proposition becomes neutered of its potency and power. We undermine everything we are supposed to be doing. We are here to help people find not the easy path but the strength to endure the hard one together. We are offering not a comfortable life but a purpose and a way out.

Now, of course, if you want to share such demands without scaring people off, people must first know something big is at stake and believe such sacrifices are worth it (which has often not been successfully communicated). But if the only reason people stick with their faith is because it's convenient, practical, helpful, fun, culturally normative, or just an otherwise nice community of people to do life with, we will eventually lose them. Why? Because living the Christian life at some point always becomes inconvenient, impractical, hard to understand, strange, and messy. And if you want your flock to make it through those times rather than drift away, they need a very big reason to stick around. It's got to be worth it.

OUR MAIN PROBLEM

Quite frankly, we don't really need to tweak our newsletter, start a new program, form a committee, or upgrade our technology. What we *need* is to rediscover our large purpose and then communicate it, reminding our flocks that the world has indeed been thrown off balance and that each of them is needed in this grand story. They have been summoned to something great, beyond their wildest imaginations. Something wonderful that compels them to engage, to act, to commit, to rearrange their lives, to sacrifice, to become saints. The Gospel message has that incredible power. As Bishop Robert Barron, founder of Word on Fire Catholic Ministries, says, "It grabs you, rearranges you, and sends you on a mission."

There are big things at stake. Does what you're doing at your church feel that way?

DREAM + REFLECT

- Imagine ten years from now. Dream big. What does your church or ministry look like?

- Why does it matter if somebody comes to your church or not?

- When living out the faith gets really hard, why should someone persevere? Why are heavy sacrifices worth it?

- Challenge: Examine your latest email to your flock or listen to your announcements this Sunday. Are the answers you listed above apparent in your communications? Are you clearly communicating where you're going, what is at stake, and why the cost is worth it? *Go to* whytheyfollow.com/goals *for a free short course on how to set big goals that will motivate your flock.*

CHAPTER FIVE

Context Matters

In the beginning, there was nothing. No time. No space. No universe. No void. No creation. There was only God. And then God said, "Let . . . me tell a story." And thus began His-story. And what a grand story it is—a love story with suspense, drama, betrayal, tragedy, epic battles, existential danger, heroic sacrifice, and the happiest ending imaginable. We are still in that story now.

Once a person sees that all of human history is really his story (God's story), it provides a context to life that can transform even the most trivial and mundane, even the worst suffering, into something deeply meaningful. This context becomes the fundamental interpretive lens through which they view everything. And through that lens, the Christian message will, of course, make much more sense.

But when somebody doesn't see history as we do, and as a result has a dramatically different way of seeing the world, communicating becomes much more challenging. If you find yourself talking past somebody, wondering how their values can be so different from yours, or failing to understand why they don't see something the way you see it, try addressing the underlying narrative first. Find out what kind of story they think they're in. Once you can agree on that, communicating becomes easier and other disagreements often go away or become easier to reconcile.

What happens, though, when an entire society stops seeing history as God's story? And instead begins telling a very different story about who we are and why we're here?

THE END OF CHRISTENDOM

Every human society has its own story it tells about itself. And though that story may or may not be rooted in truth, it still produces a kind of ruling vision—the dominant worldview of that society. This ruling vision is the lens through which most people see the world (whether they realize it's there or not), and it creates the context from within which all communicating occurs. If your message happens to resonate with that ruling vision of society, it travels easily and is accepted readily. On the other hand, when your message is dissonant and conflicts with that ruling vision, it may be met with indifference, confusion, or even outright hostility (as it threatens the status quo).

From the fourth century until recently, Western civilization essentially operated with a distinctly Christian ruling vision. This is known as the age of *Christendom*. That doesn't mean everyone always acted like good Christians, but rather that the Christian narrative and way of seeing the world was generally accepted and taken for granted. But that age is over. Even fifty years ago Archbishop Fulton Sheen was already saying, "We are at the end of Christendom. Not of Christianity, not of the Church, but of Christendom. . . . We've seen it die."

Yet many Christian leaders and institutions are still operating with a *Christendom Age* mindset—as if the ruling vision of the culture is still basically Christian. But that is no longer the case. What worked to produce thriving churches, communities, and families during an age of Christendom now suddenly doesn't work so well. What resonated with people then has now become dissonant, unconvincing, even offensive. The "ruling vision" has changed dramatically, and in a relatively short time.

Consider the following starkly different ways of seeing the world:

Christian Worldview	Modern Worldview
Life is a cosmic battle for souls.	Life is a random evolutionary process.
Freedom = able to do what God wants.	Freedom = able to do what I want.
Happiness is doing God's will.	Happiness is doing my will.
Suffering is powerful.	Suffering is to be avoided at all costs.
Cooperating with God is the ultimate adventure.	The ultimate adventure is the self-determined one.

Sacramental vision (the invisible is more important and more real).	Materialistic vision (all of reality can be detected by the natural sciences).
Our ancestors passed on to us a deep wisdom beyond our comprehension.	Moral norms and social conventions are restricting my freedom and should be torn down.
The fall and original sin are real.	Human ingenuity can build utopia on earth.
What's wrong with the world? I am.	What's wrong with the world? [Insert latest scapegoat.]

When seen in that light, it's not surprising that what resonated in an age of Christendom no longer resonates. How we run every social institution (churches, schools, and even families) must adapt. Operating in this dramatically different environment is the difference between floating with the current and swimming upstream. They require entirely different abilities and strategies. And most modern Christians are not equipped to do it, thus many of them—and even more of their children—are leaving the Church. We are now (again) in an *apostolic age*, where the ruling vision is no longer reliably Christian.

In Christendom, there is a healthy kind of maintenance necessary. But in an apostolic age, maintenance mode is suicide. We're seeing this play out before our eyes. Christian institutions chiefly concerned with maintaining what they have are shrinking. Conversely, wherever you find Christianity flourishing today, you will instead find leaders behaving with an apostolic mindset. For deeper insights into this topic, I highly recommend the book *From Christendom to Apostolic Mission: Pastoral Strategies for an Apostolic Age* from University of Mary Press.

If we are going to be successful communicators, remember that Christianity—before it is a way of life, set of doctrine, or source of wisdom—is first a way of seeing the whole of things. Much of what we say and teach simply will not resonate until we can convince people of who they truly are and the story they're actually in.

WHO AM I?

"Who I am" is the sum of everything that came before me which collaborated and conspired to produce me. Therefore, the only way to know my identity is to know my story. I may not like everything about my story so far. That's okay. Many of the best stories start with tragic beginnings.

In every story, there are some parts that are more important than others. Therefore, there are certain aspects of my identity that are far more important than others too. The most important contributing factors toward my identity may go something like this (from most important to least):

1. Religion (I'm a child of God)
2. Family/genealogy

3. Cultural heritage
4. Participation in local community groups
5. My race, gender, other physical characteristics
6. My personal preferences, past, politics, and opinions

Thus, "I'm a child of God, son of Andrew, and grandson of Frederick" are far more important parts of my identity than "I'm tall and like the peanut butter cups from Trader Joe's (the dark chocolate ones)."

But what happens to our ability to answer the question "Who am I?" when our ruling vision changes dramatically (due to things like secularization, broken families, fewer children, abortion, globalization, loss of tradition, hyper-individualism, and too much TV and social media)?

This happens:

1. ~~Religion (I'm a child of God)~~
2. ~~Family / genealogy~~
3. ~~Cultural heritage~~
4. ~~Participation in local community group~~
5. My race, gender, other physical characteristics
6. My personal preferences, past, politics, and opinions

The roles of 1–4 have been greatly diminished. And what's left are the less important parts of our identity—now made to feel like the most significant factors. No wonder we are confused and anxious. People end up trying to answer one of the most human and fundamental questions of life all on their own.

This is the original sin all over again, eating from the tree of knowledge of good and evil. It is the temptation to possess what only God can possess: the power to determine right and wrong, true and false, who I am, and what is real.

A CRISIS OF MEANING

Pleasure, power, honor, and wealth—and all of their pursuits—are just the substitutes we settle for when we've lost the real storyline. When we forget or don't understand who we are and where we fit in, it's impossible to understand the greater meaning and purpose of our lives. And so, though humans have never been more comfortable, we still have record levels of sadness and discontent. Why? We have a crisis of meaning.

Nothing motivates somebody like meaning. It's what we are all wired for. One of the key ideas of Viktor Frankl, psychiatrist and Holocaust survivor, is that "life is not primarily a quest for pleasure, as Freud believed, or a quest for power, as Alfred Adler taught, but a quest for meaning." And the problem today is that "people have enough to live by but nothing to live for; they have the means but no meaning."

Pope Benedict XVI said, "Meaning that is self-made is in the last analysis no meaning. Meaning, that is, the ground on which our existence as a totality can stand and live, cannot be made but only received." Meaning is not something we make up but something that we receive. We receive it ultimately from God, but he tells it to us as a Great Story and he uses his favorite channels to communicate it: people . . . via tradition, Scripture, prayer, history, our common identity, and leaders like you.

FINDING YOUR PLACE IN THE STORY

"I wonder what sort of tale we've fallen into?"
—Sam, *The Lord of the Rings*

If someone were to encounter Sam and Frodo on their perilous trek through Mordor (to destroy the ring of power), it would be quite obvious that they are on an important mission. It would be obvious by the tremendous effort and sacrifices they are making, their radical focus, and their willingness to put something big (their lives) at risk.

When people walk into your church, do they have the same sense about you? Do they sense that they have just encountered a group on an important mission? That they have just fallen into a great tale unfolding before them? (Try asking them!)

Furthermore, if they truly want to understand why that mission is important and where they fit into that story, they must first learn what came before. We must tell the Great Story of salvation history. What has led to this moment? Who are we? We must tell the story of the Bible, creation, Eden, the fall, why we have evil and suffering and death, the role of Israel, and finally, Jesus—conquering death and gathering the world to himself as our new King and Lord. We simply cannot understand the tale we've fallen into otherwise.

Everyone has a story of their own, each of which is part of the Great Story. You are not the author of this story. You don't have to write your own narrative. You just need to help people look up and realize what story they are already in. This is where one discovers identity, meaning, purpose, and the dragons that need slaying. Leadership is simply plugging people into their place in the Great Story. Once people realize just how epic of a tale they've fallen into, communicating your vision and leading them somewhere meaningful will be much less of a struggle.

TIPS

1. Teach them to think like Christians. Consider the table above that compares the Christian worldview with the modern worldview. Spend focused efforts explaining each of those differences (and all their implications) to your flock. Make sure they are thinking (about everything) like Christians and not just dabbling in Christianity while maintaining the modern mindset.

2. Tell the Great Story often and always. Don't assume people know the basics; many don't. And we could all use regular refreshers.
   ▸ Tell and retell the whole story of salvation history more often (and in new creative ways).
   ▸ Spend time in the whole of Scripture (Old Testament too!). And when studying any piece of Scripture, don't only focus on the immediate practical advice and implications. Make a habit of also explaining how it fits into the arc of the Great Story.

> ▸ Be careful not to reduce the faith to being mostly about spiritual advice, social justice projects, or practical insights about life. Each of those are ultimately only meaningful within the context of the Great Story.

3. Call them to action. Action is what moves stories forward. Help them enter into the Great Story at your church (and make it their own) by giving them concrete ways to participate in meaningful activities. Invite them deeper into the story (more on that in later chapters).

Take a free short course on How to Tell the Great Story at whytheyfollow.com/greatstory.

CHAPTER SIX

Why Should They Trust You?

Our Lady of Walsingham Cathedral is a beautiful, neo-Gothic style church, with corridors of stone archways, intricate stained glass, and traditional English architecture. The whole campus, let alone the church itself, exudes peace and transcendence. One day, Keri Cooper (a volunteer) came across a woman who was alone in the church. Upon further investigation, she learned the woman's home had just burned down that day. Keri approached the woman, comforted her awhile, and eventually asked the woman why she had come to the church. The woman responded, "Where else would we go?"

When Keri shared this with us later, she further reflected, "I guess if you can't go home, you go to church."

Every church leader wants their people to feel this way about their church. A beautiful and peaceful place. A transcendent space that elevates our hearts and minds. A place where God's presence is found and felt in a special way. A stable community I can always rely on to welcome me and help me bear my burdens. A space filled with friendly faces that I trust, my tribe, a second home, a lifeboat. The place I go when I can't go home.

When people have a church like that, they instinctually seek it out when they feel lost, they're looking for answers, or times get tough. But how does a church become such a place? How do we communicate that we *are* such a place?

In chapter 2, we discussed how the Gallup research found that what people want most from the leaders they follow is hope, trust, compassion, and stability. We already covered hope in earlier chapters, as it springs forth from understanding what's at stake and the Great Story we're in. Now we turn to trust, compassion, and stability (*compassion* and *stability* often contributing largely to the *trust* part). How do we communicate that we are trustworthy, compassionate, and stable?

TRUST AND DISCIPLESHIP

Sherry Weddell's brilliant book *Forming Intentional Disciples* highlights the importance of trust as the essential first step to making a disciple. She provides five thresholds of conversion: initial trust, spiritual curiosity, spiritual openness, spiritual seeking, and, ultimately, intentional discipleship.

Without trust, it is very difficult, if not impossible, for a person to progress through the other thresholds. They will not have a safe space to be curious and ask vulnerable questions. They will not feel safe putting themselves into a place of openness to a radically different way of seeing the world. And they will not see you as a reliable partner as they seek answers to deeper questions. That's why they say, "People don't care how much you know until they know how much you care." They must trust that you care about them first.

If you want them to follow you somewhere, to achieve some vision, then they must also trust that you are capable of getting them there. That includes trusting both that you'll do what you say you'll do and also that you'll take care of them along the way. People buy into the leader before they buy into the vision. Before they will hear the other things you want to tell them or follow you anywhere, they must trust you, the leader, first.

ABOVE REPROACH

First Timothy 3:1–13 gives a long list of wise qualifications for leaders in the church. But it begins with the need for the person to be "above reproach"—that is, their trustworthiness is so evident it cannot be questioned. I don't believe it is listed first simply by coincidence, as trust is foundational to the effectiveness of the leader. Aristotle even went so far as to say that "character may almost be called the most effective means of communication."

Trust is hard earned and easily broken. It takes a long time to build it up and only a single moment to break it down. If we don't have trust, we won't be able to communicate our message and make disciples. The devil uses this to his advantage. So we must be even more on guard not to allow lapses in judgment that diminish trust from our flock. If the devil can destroy this one thing, he knows he can undermine everything.

Being above reproach involves going above and beyond what is expected of the average person or organization, and it takes a rare kind of maturity. It's more than just doing what is right and avoiding what is wrong.

Good person = doing what is right.
Wise leader = avoiding even the appearance of doing something wrong.
Above reproach = demonstrating a level of character that makes wrongdoing unimaginable.

With that in mind, all churches should implement and make known official policies and procedures that keep leadership above reproach. This includes:

- financial checks and balances,
- safe environment policies,
- operational transparency,
- open and proactive communication, and
- personal rules for leaders that will minimize temptation, avoid the appearance of potential wrongdoing, and prevent even the possibility of bad behavior.

SMELLING LIKE THE SHEEP

"You call me Teacher and Lord—and you are right,
for that is what I am. So if I, your Lord and Teacher,
have washed your feet, you also ought to
wash one another's feet."

—John 13:13–14

How far are you willing to go to walk with the people you lead? Are you neck deep in their issues like a good neighbor should be? Do you understand them, love them as yourself, and help shoulder their burdens? Are we taking time to care for each other and wash each other's feet?

We must not be so busy that we, as Pope Francis says, no longer smell like our sheep. A good leader smells like the sheep. That means spending lots of time with them—that's it. There are no shortcuts.

COMPASSION

The word *compassion* comes from two Latin words: *com* (with) and *pati* (to suffer). Compassion literally means "to suffer with." It's not just feeling bad for somebody worse off than you. It's not hoping things get better for them. It's not sharing the hashtag or buying the bumper sticker. It is doing what Jesus commands in the second part of the Great Commandment: to love our neighbor as ourselves. It is more than merely wishing them well. It means if they have a problem, it is now my problem to help shoulder too. If they are suffering, we enter into that experience in a real way and *suffer* with them.

STABILITY

Stability is an interesting, and perhaps unexpected, characteristic to pop out of the Gallup leadership study—though it makes a lot of sense. It is directly related to trust. What does it mean to offer stability as a leader?

First, it means you do what you say you're going to do. Is your word stable? Can people depend on you? And does your track record demonstrate it? If you are always talking about ideas but never doing them, people will stop following. This applies to the big vision but perhaps just as importantly to the everyday little things.

Second, it means you're consistent. Do people know what to expect? Are you thoughtful about your goals and steady in your march toward accomplishing them? Or are you frequently changing your goals and chasing something new?

Third, when it comes to your church, it means you are rooted in something bigger and deeper than just your own ideas. Is your vision bigger than one personality? Do your beliefs, practices, and traditions transcend the shifting whims of modernity?

A lot of the Church's efforts over the past half-century (and beyond) to be more "relevant" have been inauthentic and unnatural developments, abruptly divorced from the traditions that came before (both in how we worship and in how we live our lives). People, by nature, don't trust that kind of rupture. It communicates an inauthenticity, instability, and uncertainty—like this organization doesn't really know who they are. That's not something people ultimately feel confident following, so much so that people have left the faith faster instead. As G.K. Chesterton said, "We do not really want a religion that is right where we are right. What we want is a religion that is right where we are wrong." And again: "We do not want, as the newspapers say, a Church that will move with the world. We want a Church that will move the world."

Our unity as Christians is central to this issue as well. The more divided we are amongst ourselves, the more we communicate to the world an instability that people will be hesitant to trust and follow. Jesus prayed for us in John 17:21 "that they may all be one. As you, Father, are in me and I am in you, may they also be in us, so that the world may believe that you have sent me." Jesus tells us what needs to happen if we want the world to believe. We should take that seriously and constantly work to resolve our differences with goodwill and charity.

REPAIRING RELATIONSHIPS

"I never apologize. . . . I'm sorry, but that's the way I am."
—Homer Simpson

It probably wasn't your fault, but you may still need to apologize for it. To your flock, you represent the Church. That's part of what it means to be a leader. You get to be the face of a very complex, beautiful, amazing, wonderful, mysterious Body of Christ, sometimes represented by a bunch of knuckleheads or even disgraceful, broken sinners who do awful things.

Leaders take responsibility when things go wrong and pass on the credit when things go right. That's the job. Sometimes that means apologizing on behalf of us all for things that weren't your fault. This could be anything from a serious scandal to something as seemingly trivial as previously misusing someone's contact information (perhaps why they are hesitant to give you their cell phone number now).

The good news is that genuine, contrite apologies are powerful and go a long way. At a minimum, they're a necessary first step toward the healing many people need before they can begin trusting again and progressing in discipleship.

STARTING THE CYCLE OF TRUST

The ritual of the handshake dates back to ancient times and is a universal gesture of trust. It's a way to show an adversary, "I'm unarmed and making myself vulnerable to you. You can trust me." That creates an opportunity for a cycle of trust to begin.

When you put something at risk in leading your people, a similar opportunity occurs. Maybe you're risking your physical life, but more often it's your reputation, your career, or your pride, through potential embarrassment, failure, or criticism. At the end of the day, however, how much you are willing to risk communicates—louder than anything else—just how much you believe in the cause and care about your people. It shows them you are willing to put the interests of the tribe ahead of your own. If you are willing to risk something for them, maybe they will risk something in return. That's when big things start to happen.

Approach your people defenseless and vulnerable. Trust them first. Stand vulnerable on the battlefield and boldly ask them to join you in doing something big—something that might not work. Show them that you are willing to put something of your own at risk, be criticized, make tough decisions, protect them, and patiently earn their trust. Do you believe enough to put something big at stake? If it means one more person would come to believe? See what happens when you believe that much.

TRUSTING IN THEMSELVES

Finally, as if it's not hard enough already to earn their trust in you, a leader's job is also to convince people to believe and trust in themselves. Sadly, low self-esteem seems more rampant than ever.

But an encouraging word from any church leader has great power to radically change a person's mentality. It may be the critical first step along the path to discipleship.

Your people want to know if they have what it takes to do something big and meaningful in this world. But it often requires a leader—typically a father, mother, boss, pastor, mentor, or someone with authority in their lives—to tell them, "Yes, you have what it takes. We need you. You are loved and play an important role in this Great Story. Follow me."

SELF-ASSESSMENT

Score yourself from 1–10 on each:

- How smelly are you? (I mean when it comes to smelling like your sheep!)

- How well do you operate "above reproach"?

- How much does the average person in the pew trust you?

- How well do you currently "suffer with" your people?

- How well do you use your influence to personally encourage people?

CHAPTER SEVEN

Cultivating Soil

When planting crops, a good farmer knows the actual casting of the seeds is the easiest part. The real work—and the biggest factor in success—is in the preparation of the soil. It's easy to think we're just supposed to scatter seeds, but much of our work of communicating is in cultivating soil.

Why does the mission grab hold of some people much easier than others? How can the same message bear fruit so differently from one person to the next? The parable of the sower (Matthew 13) tells us the answer quite clearly: bad soil (rocky ground and thorns). C.S. Lewis put it another way, saying that God "shows much more of himself to some people than to others—not because he has favorites, but because it is impossible for him to show himself to a man whose whole mind and character are in the wrong condition."

George Bernard Shaw, the playwright and atheist, is said to have remarked that the single biggest problem in communication is the illusion that it has taken place. We think that because we've said it (casted seeds), it's been communicated. We think that because it's not bearing fruit, we must be saying it wrong. But sometimes the problem is just bad soil.

Fixing this means understanding what has put people's "whole mind and character in the wrong condition" in the first place. What has contaminated and sterilized the soil? Here are some answers:

Poor formation: This is one of the direct explanations Jesus gives us in the parable of the sower as to why some are unable to receive the Gospel—they hear the word but don't understand. As Bishop Barron often preaches, we must stop dumbing down the faith! Christians need to rediscover our deep, rich intellectual tradition, built upon thousands of years of accumulated wisdom handed down by the most brilliant humans to ever live. And we must figure out how to pass it down to our children. Otherwise, the faith will not take root and bear fruit, because *they will not understand*. We need more rigorous religious education and, more importantly, families that fully and authentically integrate the faith into their daily lives.

Social instability: Some people initially respond positively to our message, but it doesn't last because the instability of their lives keeps it from taking root. Broken families, divided local communities, and a lack of social rootedness have taken away the like-minded social support needed to stick with it when times get tough. Therefore, people eventually slip back into their old ways and whatever the crowd around them is doing.

Oversimplification: When we dumb down the faith so that it fits into our own overly neat, black-and-white boxes and leave no room for the complexities and mysteries of this life, people end up with a flattened, inauthentic version of Christianity that will not stand up to experience. St. Augustine said, "Si comprehendis, non est Deus" (If you understand, it is not God).

A modern lack of imagination: The great decline in faith today coincides with a great decline in imagination. Modern man increasingly finds it hard to believe in anything that the natural sciences can't detect or measure. But of course, limiting one's view of reality to only what our little inventions and funny instruments can measure is absurd and unreasonable. As Hamlet said, there are more things in heaven and earth than we could ever dream of. But many people can't see them. Why? Because it takes a healthy imagination to see what our eyes cannot—to see what is really there. (Read Peter Kreeft's fantastic book *Doors in the Walls of the World* for a brilliantly reasoned exploration of this.)

People have been hurt: They've been scandalized, betrayed, and let down—particularly by the people they love, other Christians, and their own church. Whether it is personal wounds, larger scandals, or even just a generally bad previous experience with a church, everything we say and do is filtered through the lens of that wounded past.

People are not rational: As much as we tell ourselves that we are rational thinkers, the fact remains that we are very much emotional actors. We say we are just looking for "the facts" but tend to only seek out the facts that affirm what we already believe. The most successful marketers and politicians know that passion is what sells, not logic. They know that people don't believe the best ideas; they believe the easiest ones to understand or the ones they already want to believe. Reason rarely moves people to action and sacrifice—emotion does. Emotion leads to motion. And though emotion alone is not a reliable gauge of what is true, it is beautiful and human nonetheless and should be part of the equation when communicating.

Blindness to the familiar: The fumes of Christianity have remained so nominally and culturally present that the post-Christian modern American assumes he's already heard every-thing we have to say (though he hasn't) and knows what he's rejecting (though he doesn't). G.K. Chesterton, in his classic book *Everlasting Man*, contends that such a person is in fact the worst judge of Christianity, "the ill-educated Christian turning gradually into the ill-tempered agnostic, entangled in the end of a feud of which he never understood the beginning, blighted with a sort of hereditary boredom with he knows not what, and already weary of hearing what he has never heard." The skeptics say they want to see miracles, but what they really want is something new. The familiar, though miraculous, is perceived as irrelevant. In this age, nothing causes a person to tune something out more quickly than finding it familiar—believing they've already heard it all before.

The problem of suffering: One of the biggest reasons people lose their faith is they can't believe a loving God would allow innocent people to suffer. When they experience innocent people suffering (an emotional and heart-wrenching reality that hardens hearts), they conclude therefore that a loving God cannot exist. It's unsound logic, but it's emotionally persuasive and must be dealt with if we want the rest of our message to be heard. We know we are in the middle of a Great Story that ends happily ever after and that God doesn't create evil but allows it so that some greater good may come from it. We know that suffering is somehow mysteriously meaningful. Peter Kreeft gives four answers to this problem of evil that every church leader should know—check them out at whytheyfollow.com/evil.

Admittedly, many of these issues are particularly frustrating to acknowledge because they are complex and difficult to solve. Some we can directly address now, some will take generations to improve, and still others are simply part of our nature that we must account for when communicating. Regardless, it's critical that (1) we set realistic expectations and understand that successful communication may require the long, difficult job of cultivating soil first, and (2) we begin solving these now so that the next generation of leaders may produce more from their soil than we have from ours.

REFLECT

- What are three things you could start doing this year to improve the soil in your community?

CHAPTER EIGHT

Navigating the Digital Landscape

While other churches were busy putting more and more things onto their websites, Cristina Folan was actually taking some things off of hers. As the Director of Communications and Evangelization at Notre Dame of Mt. Carmel Church, she admits they had gotten "carried away with putting everything online." She confessed further, "I was guilty of that. We put the whole registration process onto our website. People could go there, click, and become a parishioner. We wouldn't even see them. We didn't even have a chance to greet them."

She still uses the website to get new people plugged in, but now instead it steers people (if interested) to come in and meet in person. And instead of just telling them about the church and what they need to do to join, she invites them into a conversation and asks them about themselves first. She gets to know them. Then she can personalize what she offers based on their particular needs, find ways to put their unique talents to use, or sometimes just listen. She says, "They are often suffering and just need to be listened to . . . not sold to about what you want them to do or told our agenda for them."

Cristina's story is a powerful example of both the pitfalls and opportunities of the digital era. New technologies offer us powerful ways to improve our ministries. But it is absolutely critical to understand that—though it will solve some—technology will not solve most of our biggest problems in the Church today. In fact, if the flock is drifting away or not engaging now, wielding powerful technologies may just drive them away faster. The focus on new tools can sometimes mask or distract from more fundamental communication and leadership issues that really need to be addressed first.

Regardless, we still have to figure out how to navigate this rapidly changing, ever-present digital landscape. So here is some guidance that will help you avoid its detours while also making the most of its tremendous opportunities.

BE INTENTIONAL

Known for their extremely low-tech, simple way of life, the Amish actually have a lot to teach us about technology use. Contrary to what many think, the Amish are not anti-technology. They are just very thoughtful about what technology they use and why. They are willing to forego using a very helpful technology if they believe that it undermines their more important goals and values (like keeping the family and community healthy and strong). They look at each piece of technology and ask, Will this cause more harm than good? Will it undermine the stability of families or the traditions important to passing on our way of life? Are we more likely to become this technology's master or its slave? They look at the whole picture, and we should do the same.

It might make sense to embrace a technology that makes it easier to accept a payment, send and receive messages with lots of people, manage a member database, register for events from home, easily access information, among many others. Technology can improve every one of these tasks, freeing you to lead more effectively and achieve more with fewer resources. But it's not always that simple. Has your church ever solved one department's administrative problem only to end up making other people's jobs harder? Sometimes technology solves one problem only to create others. Beyond that, all of its effects may not be immediately evident—gradually or quietly perpetuating unhealthy lifestyles, exploiting privacy, reducing opportunities to build relationships, dehumanizing interactions, and the like. An intentional and holistic approach is required.

ASKING THE RIGHT QUESTION

Given the many ways technology has clearly improved some aspects of life, it's easy to start assuming that technology always makes everything better, or that newer is always better, or that somehow all of our human problems will one day be solved by technology as it advances (they won't). For all the good technology does do, thus far, the rapid advancement of technology has coincided with a rapid decline in family stability, a great loss of faith, fewer close friendships, and an increase in depression and anxiety. We are more likely to spend five minutes talking to a stranger online than to our neighbor next door (who we are commanded to care for as ourselves). And perhaps never before in history has a generation so unsuccessfully passed on the faith to the next generation, their own children. We should proceed with caution.

The question to answer is not "How can the Church *win* in the digital landscape?" Such thinking can end up morphing the Church into something that competes on that turf but is no longer good at being the Church. What does it profit a man to win Twitter but lose his flock?

Instead, we should turn that question around and ask, "In what ways can these digital tools help us to be a better Church?" Then we can thoughtfully apply only what helps us, throwing the rest in the digital recycle bin.

THE MYTH THAT THESE TOOLS ARE "NEUTRAL"

"Pay no attention to that man behind the curtain!"
—The Great Oz

Many of today's digital tools (especially those claiming to be "free") have somebody behind the curtain managing a dopamine drip that influences your behavior. Unfortunately, their priority is not to make you a more virtuous person and help you get to heaven. Some of the smartest people in the world are building systems to hijack our psyches and exploit our vices in order to sell us more stuff and get us to scroll just a little bit longer. They tell you it's "free" to use, but it's really not. Seth Godin, the world-renowned marketing expert, reminds us, "If you aren't paying for it, you aren't the customer. You're the product."

This isn't cynical, Big Tech, dystopian conspiracy theory. It's the normal, accepted way that just about every social media platform is designed to operate. (Check out the documentary *The Social Dilemma* for an eye-opening exploration of this.) As people chiefly concerned with the souls of our flock, this reality should weigh heavily as we consider the use of such platforms.

Regardless, it is not wise to invest too much in social media platforms where you don't own the connection (the ability to reach your people) in the end. They are constantly trying to insert advertisements between you and your members, make you pay extra to reach your people, or censor you when they disagree with what you say. There are simpler, smarter, better communication channels out there (discussed more in later chapters).

CONFLATING ALL DIGITAL TOOLS WITH SOCIAL MEDIA

It's also important not to conflate every tool of the digital age with "social media." There are many software tools and new technologies (sometimes more broadly referred to as the "new media") that can help churches operate more efficiently and effectively: websites, email, texting, Zoom, endless apps, video streaming, podcasts, church management software, online giving, event registration, and a rapidly growing list of other software and hardware that can transform how we do things in positive ways. While some do have an important social dimension, they have little to do, necessarily, with the various social media platforms of today. So don't lump them all together or treat them all the same. They are neither all good nor all bad.

THE MEGAPHONE MISTAKE

The opportunity of the digital age is not that you get to yell louder. It's not a shinier, louder megaphone. That mindset worked (sort of) in the early days of the internet and was a holdover from the age of broadcast media. But the megaphone approach doesn't work anymore because everyone has one. Now it's just noisy.

For local churches, the power of the internet is not as a megaphone. It's in its network effect and its capacity for ideas and information to spread quickly. What used to be expensive or take months to spread by word of mouth can now happen in minutes for pennies. Information has potential to spread very quickly—if people find it valuable. So the question for the local church is not "What can we shout louder so people pay attention?" It's "What can we whisper that will spread?"

In the age of digital connectivity, if it doesn't spread when you whisper it, don't waste time shouting it on eleven different channels. Fix what you're saying first, and then you won't have to shout.

AUTOMATION IS FOR ROBOTS, NOT RELATIONSHIPS

Michael Scott, Regional Manager of Dunder Mifflin in the popular sitcom *The Office*, is known for his genius—though often accidental—insights into leadership. One episode in particular highlights the dangers of trusting technology too much. While blindly following the instructions of his vehicle's GPS navigation system, Michael obediently drives his car directly into a lake. He later humorously reflects on his experience and what he's learned, saying, "People will never be replaced by machines. In the end, life and business are about human connections . . . and computers are about trying to murder you in a lake. And to me the choice is easy."

You can't talk long about technology and communications without soon coming to the topic of automation. Technology, particularly software, is transforming the world, making it more efficient and allowing us to do things we could never have dreamed of doing. This is good news for churches when it helps us operate more efficiently and better steward our resources. Let's take an example of something we deal with a lot at Flocknote: communicating a message to a large group of people quickly.

Getting a message to a thousand people (which many of our churches regularly do) would take a lot of time and effort without software that can blast a text message or email to the entire flock all at once in minutes. This is a helpful kind of automation. Would it be better if you spoke to each person individually with a personalized message? Sometimes, sure. But that is usually impossible, and most people don't need (or have time for) a personal conversation every time information needs to exchange hands. That's an automation win.

On the other hand, some automations can actually do more harm than good. One common example can occur with automated follow-ups, whether it is an automated new visitor welcome text message campaign, or an automated happy birthday message, or any kind of message that pretends to be personal (when it's not). Have you ever gotten a letter in the mail that looked like somebody had hand-written it, but you eventually realized it was just an advertising trick? Or perhaps you've gotten an email that addressed you by name and appeared to be a message sent only to you, but you later realized it was just an automated bulk email to lots of people pretending to be a personal message?

Once people realize these messages are automated (and that you weren't really personally thinking of them), they not only mean little but can actually harm the relationship. If people can already tell something is automated, then they just feel spammed or treated like a number in a system. If you do manage to trick them into thinking it's a genuinely personal message, that's even worse. Not only do we not want to be misleading, but people almost always eventually find out anyway. And once they do, they feel lied to and tricked.

Those kinds of automations just aren't necessary anyway. Such tactics may work (sort of) when marketing to strangers, but it is no way to build quality, long-term relationships with people you care about. Not only can it come off icky and spammy, but it's not why engaged followers open your email anyway. They open your email because they are part of the tribe, because they've bought into the mission and the story and can't wait to find out what happens next!

So yes, automate communications to the whole group. Automate registration and form capture. Automate recurring giving. Automate inter-office workflow tracking. Automate tedious tasks around the office that free you up to do more important and meaningful things. But don't automate relationships. Don't automate welcoming people and engaging them. Don't automate wishing somebody a happy birthday! Don't automate anything that risks undermining the trust of a person. And certainly don't automate anything that gives away an opportunity to build a more personal relationship with a member of the flock. That's the ministry. That's what moves the needle. That's the part that takes you being a human. Let the robots do the rest if you must, but not that. Otherwise, you may find yourself driving into a lake.

WHAT THEY DON'T NEED

Our people don't actually need to spend more time online. They don't need more posts to read on social media. A week has 168 hours. The average person already spends about 77 hours of that on a screen or device (and another 47.6 hours/week sleeping). They don't need something else to look at and compete for their attention online.

Don't misunderstand me: the greater Church needs a digital presence and to compete on this key battleground of ideas. And certain leaders and ministries, God bless them, are uniquely called to that space. But I think we greatly exaggerate the amount of time and effort a local church should invest into interacting online. We think it's the next best thing, but most of it is a poor use of time.

We know families are suffering from brokenness, lack of social stability, anxiety, fewer close friends, and disconnection from extended family. What people need is to look at the person in front of them. To be present with their children. To pray together as a family. To look their neighbor in the eye. To eat dinner around a table and talk about their day with each other. The last thing they need from their local church is more stuff to do online. Instead of adding to the noise, we should help our flocks find peace amidst it.

THE HOLE IN THE BUCKET

When you have a giant hole in your bucket, you don't go running around trying to fill the bucket up faster. First, you fix the hole. You saw the statistics from chapter 1. People are leaving Christianity at faster and faster rates. There is a giant hole in the bucket.

For most churches, the people we need to reach most are not faceless usernames somewhere out there on the internet. Rather, they are sitting in front of us, in the flesh. You probably even know their names. And they're already giving you at least some attention. Maybe not every Sunday, but some Sundays. The imminent crisis (and opportunity) is that the people who still call themselves Christian (and are *still showing up sometimes*) are becoming less engaged and gradually drifting away.

The urgency for the *local church*, then, is not to run out looking for more people online. It's to first stop wasting the attention that the people we already have are already giving us and to figure out what we will do or say the next time we see them that's going to get them leaning in rather than drifting out. If you want to build a raging fire of a ministry, the kindling is already sitting in the pews!

Church leaders have very limited time. Instead of an hour on social media today, I guarantee that hour would be better spent figuring out what to say to those "same old people" the next time they show up. What will you do that will grab them by the lapels and get them excited about what it is that you're doing here?

AN EMBODIED CHURCH

Another dangerous temptation of the digital age is to start believing the Church itself can be digital. Some have even said that for churches "attendance is not decreasing, it is decentralizing." That is a huge concern.

The Church is corporeal. We are embodied souls, not souls trapped in bodies. The Church is sacramental, anointing with oil, baptizing with water, where two or three are gathered, eat my flesh, drink my blood, do this in memory of me. The Church has a physical body, as Christ has a physical body. It quite simply does not exist as data-bits and ideas, nor as merely spiritual, nor as decentralized bodies. The Body of Christ is a real, unified body. It is not just a spiritual symbol of our solidarity but a physical, mysterious reality.

Yes, real communication and ministry can be done digitally. But to be the Church is to come together in the flesh. Humans were not made to be in digital, disembodied relationships. And there will continue to be negative consequences if we rely on them too much.

THE GOOD NEWS

The Church, by its nature, is missionary. St. Paul went out to the Areopagus to engage the Athenian intellectual elites on their home turf. St. Thomas was called to the Far East to proclaim the Gospel in very foreign lands. The Church must be willing to go out and meet the world, engaging it on its turf, and sharing the Gospel. The internet has been called a "Digital Areopagus." It is where much of the public debate is happening with the world.

So yes, we must have people and ministries who are called to go there and bring Christ, fight for a seat at the table, and compete in that marketplace of ideas. It's also a powerful means of providing resources, inspiration, and leadership to the faithful. We desperately need such leaders. But the real urgency for local ministry is not there. It is largely offline, with a focus on the familiar faces in the pews and down the street—not looking for strangers on the internet. You actually don't need very many tools to lead a thriving church. And you certainly don't have to feel overwhelmed by the perpetually changing digital landscape. After all, people don't follow you because you're tech-savvy, on the latest social platform, and understand the latest technological tips and tricks. They follow you because they want to go where you are going and they believe that you can get them there. Because something they care about is at stake.

REFLECT

- What are you doing at your church that is so good you could whisper it and it would spread?

- Look at how much time and money you're putting into each communication channel vs. the fruit it produces. Which ones are most worth the effort?

PART II

PRACTICAL LESSONS

CHAPTER NINE

How to Add Followers

Once upon a time, you could just put an announcement in the bulletin and everyone got the message. (I'm not sure that's true, but it's a nice beginning to a fairy tale.) But then they stopped reading the bulletin. So we started reading the bulletin to them after Mass on Sunday. Then they started leaving early because the announcements were too long. So we moved the announcements to during the homily, thinking, "Aha! Finally, now they are forced to listen!" But, of course, that didn't work either.

Then the digital age dawned. We said, "Ah, now we can send information to them in many wonderful ways. Now they will listen!" So we posted on our website, but few people visited. We posted on every social media network, but only eleven people liked it. Then we emailed it, but many didn't open it. We emailed it again (and again). And fewer opened it still. Then we texted them to let them know we sent them an email. And many unsubscribed.

The lesson we've hopefully learned by now? You can't make them listen. Begging is no good either.

BEGGING THEM TO LISTEN

If you're always begging for somebody's attention, they aren't really a follower. Just because you have somebody's email address or phone number does not make them a follower. Just because they like your Facebook page (and Facebook says they're your follower) does not mean they are following you. Just because they received a sacrament from you, or visited a long time ago, or show up in your database does not make them a follower. And while you may be able to reach them, it doesn't mean you've earned the right to be heard.

The "please listen to me" posture does not attract followers. When we resend the same message multiple times and copy and paste that same message over multiple channels, particularly with little signs of engagement, that comes off as desperate. It communicates to them that what we are saying must not be that valuable (since nobody seems to want it).

You shouldn't go to the other extreme and play "hard to get." Just be aware that desperate pleas and spammy reminders communicate the wrong message. Even if it works in the short term, you're more likely to get tuned out next time. Instead, the better rule is, see what happens when you whisper. Do people lean in and ask you to repeat yourself? That's how you know if you've earned it.

WHAT HAVE YOU EARNED?

Darryl: Hey Andy.
Andy: Hey Darryl.
Darryl: You gotta stop texting me so much.
Andy: But I wanted you to know that Michael and I are
wearing the same tie today. It's insane.
Darryl: You need to change your standard for what's
worthy of a text. Ask yourself, "Is this something Darryl
needs to know?" The answer's almost always no.
Andy: Got it. Then I will call you.
Darryl: No.

—The Office

One of the most common questions we get from church leaders is "How often should I be sending out information to people? How much is too much?" It's an important question. But the answer is not a simple, straightforward answer (once a week, etc.). A more important question should be answered first: *What have you earned?*

How often should a spammer communicate with you? Zero often, right? Why? Because they haven't earned the right to talk to you. How often can your mom call you? Every five minutes if she wants. She's your mom! She's earned it.

When, years ago, we started our viral "Read the *Catechism* / Gospel in a Year" email lists and hundreds of thousands of people signed up to get a daily email, we earned the right to send an email

... every day. When somebody joins your weekly Bible study for the spring, you earn the right to communicate probably once a week or so for the spring, then a few more times over the next year to follow up or invite them to the next one.

How much you've earned is not always obvious, but the concept remains. How much you should communicate depends on what you've earned. The answer to that will be different depending on the group and its purpose, your relationship, the quality of the content (the better it is, the more you earn), the importance and urgency of the topic, and the extent to which somebody has opted in.

That makes it especially challenging when communicating with mixed groups (i.e., your weekly email newsletter sent to the whole community). You may have people who are so engaged that they would love to hear from you every day. Most people will be annoyed by that though. If you haven't earned permission to send them something every day, you'll drive them away or they'll tune you out.

By the way, for a church's regular newsletter, a weekly pulse tends to be most natural. Churches meet weekly, and most people find it very reasonable that if they've joined your church, you would keep them updated with the most important stuff each week.

Every situation is different, though the same principle applies to everything we communicate. We have to earn the right to lead them. We earn the right to more of their time and attention. We earn permission to speak again tomorrow. We earn the right to be heard. If we haven't earned it, that's called "spam."

ENROLLMENT VS. ENFORCEMENT

If you use your authority or influence to get compliance or have to mandate what people do, you're using *enforcement*, not *enrollment*. Enforcement works for legal matters. It works (to some extent) in the military, at work, or in schools, where there is a chain of command to which people agree. Although, if that's all you have, it's questionable how well it really "works" at achieving the ultimate goals. But it does "work" in the sense that those who sign up for that tend to comply.

On the other hand, it doesn't work well with voluntary communities (like churches) and especially not with evangelization. Regardless, we don't want compliant proles; we want enthusiastic, engaged followers. The only way to get that is with enrollment (not enforcement).

When I'm "enrolled" in the cause, I'm not just here in body; my heart is in it too. I don't just *have* to be here; I *want* to be here. It means I actually want to go where you are going and believe you can get me there. It means "I'm in." Whatever is at stake must be something people care enough about. It's really that simple. And if they don't care enough yet, we have to either (1) begin with something they care about, or (2) convince them to care. If we skip this step of getting people enrolled in our cause, our task of leading and communicating becomes exhausting and Sisyphean.

FIRST, GET TEN.

Let's say you get ten people to show up this week, but you wish you had one hundred. Our immediate inclination, then, is to figure out how to *promote* what we are doing to more people to increase attendance—blast it out on as many channels as we can or come up with a fun video to advertise what we're doing. This is the wrong way to do it.

Don't look first at the ninety people who didn't show up—look at the ten who did. Are those ten people truly enrolled in the cause? What did the ten think? What did they do? Did they leave changed, inspired, and excited to tell all their friends?

If not, focus on achieving that before promoting further. Turn those ten into committed followers. Once you do that, the ten will do all the promotion you need, and you'll be at one hundred in no time.

Seth Godin described this principle over ten years ago while giving advice on building a following online. This principle applies just as much (if not more so) to building church communities (Jesus started with twelve, remember?). First, get a small group of people who don't just show up but are truly *fired up* about what you're doing and can't wait to tell everyone else about it.

GROW BY REFERRAL

There were many reasons why Flocknote decided to quit advertising (and social media) altogether. Yes, we were sick of the way personal data gets abused and used to manipulate people and sell them things, and we didn't want to support such a corrupt system. We were leery of the dangers of Big Tech and the legitimate threat it poses to free speech, the propagation of the truth, and the economy as a whole (part of why we decided to become employee-owned as well). And we knew that giving all that up would mean missed opportunities and slower growth. From a business perspective, it looked crazy. We didn't care. Besides, we really love growing by referral. It means, generally, we only grow (get new churches signing up) if we've taken exceptional care of the customers God has already given us. It is the healthiest, most stable, and most responsible kind of growth. We love it and haven't looked back.

Church communities grow best by referrals too—not by ads or big promotions or mass communication. If you're not doing something your current people are excited enough to tell their friends about and invite more people into, then fix that first. Once that is fixed, growth takes care of itself. If you try it the other way around (getting lots of people coming in the door without creating something they love yet), you create a revolving door of people coming in the front and drifting out the back, and you'll be perpetually plagued by many other frustrations and unnecessary problems as a result.

Stop thinking of your media and communications as, primarily, a way to get bigger. Instead, think of them as a way to go deeper with your community and to accomplish something big together (execute). If you do that well, you'll grow. Give people something worth sharing and talking about and they will. Insist on growing by referrals.

HOW TO BUILD A RAGING FIRE

Have you ever tried to catch fire to a huge bonfire? If you simply hold a match up to a large log, of course the match burns out long before the log catches fire. Alternatively, if you simply move the match around, lighting every clump of dry leaves in the pile on fire, you end up wasting all your leaves—burning them up before they have a chance to catch anything else on fire. No, to build a raging fire, you start small and focus on one spot.

First, you gather some dry leaves and other kindling in a single, small pile, and you add some very small twigs on top. Now when you light it up, the small twigs begin to catch fire and burn. You gently blow air (oxygen) onto the small fire, helping it to burn better. Then you add more kindling and small twigs, still blowing gently as you go. As that grows, you begin adding medium-sized sticks. As those catch fire, you add slightly bigger branches. Eventually, bigger and bigger logs are added, now aided by your leaf-blower blasting air across the newly forming coals, until you end up with a giant bonfire, raging and consuming anything that touches it.

That's how you grow (or revive) your church or ministry. The lighted match is your proclamation of the Gospel. The wood is your flock. The gusts of air are prayer. And (if you'll allow me to risk taking my analogy too far) any moisture in the wood is the noise of the world, whereas dryness (i.e., nicely-seasoned wood) is silence, which allows God's voice to be heard. Gasoline (a dangerous way to do it, by the way) would be the saints and the martyrs (a dangerously compelling way to live).

That's how you build a raging fire of a ministry. You start small and you focus. Spread your efforts too thin, try to reach too many people at once (i.e., "everyone"), or attempt to do too many things, and you'll wear yourself out starting fires that keep going out. Instead, aim for intensity before scale.

NATURAL LIMITS OF COMMUNITY GROWTH

The earliest hunter-gatherer tribes of humans maxed out between 100 to 150 people. It's similar with individual Native American tribes, the bushman of South Africa, Amish communities, even marine companies. Professor Robin Dunbar of Oxford University did further study to see if this idea also applied to what number of people worked most efficiently together, particularly in a manufacturing facility. He discovered the same thing: 150 was the magic number. It seems people begin struggling to manage more than about 150 relationships in various contexts.

Once communities grow beyond these natural human limits, there is increased abstraction. People become less engaged and feel less connection to the tribe, less ownership for the group, and less individual responsibility for helping achieve the mission. If we dare grow bigger and remain a healthy, thriving organization, hard work is needed to overcome this natural human dynamic. Otherwise, we risk having large portions of the group become disengaged.

The data on church communities bears this out. The average-sized church community in the United States, across all denominations, is around 100 to 150 people. And in communities that grow significantly bigger, they tend to have large portions that are disengaged (and drifting away). Interestingly enough, if you look at how many people in those larger churches are still highly engaged, it often ends up (guess where?) around 100 to 150 people or families.

Does this mean we can't or shouldn't aspire to lead larger groups? No. The Church itself, along with many of its individual communities, is of course an organism much larger than this. But it does mean that growing beyond these natural limits (*and* keeping people engaged) won't happen easily on its own. More skilled and effective leadership is required, including these three things:

1. **A culture of communicating the big vision.** The big vision creates a unity of purpose across an otherwise very diverse collection of subgroups within the larger community. Everyone shares

it in common no matter their other differences, and powerful and personal connections are forged even between strangers. You may not know all the faces and names, but you know you're all in the same boat, rowing in the same direction to achieve the same goal you all care deeply about.

2. Cultivation of smaller groups within the larger group. I'm not only referring to "small groups" as we normally think of them, which can be helpful too. I'm referring to any smaller social circles within the larger community (friend groups, particular ministries, and other various cultural and social subgroups) that are strong in themselves. Some people may call this "cliquey" and dissuade them from existing because they can feel closed off to the larger group and unwelcoming to visitors. Those are real concerns to balance. But all in all, groups-within-the-group are healthy and essential features of any stable large human community. The key, of course, is having #1 above—a culture of communicating the big vision (something more important that unifies all groups).

3. Transcendent leadership. When the community is first starting and still small, leaders often carry people on their backs, muscling things forward and making things happen. But when they're successful and things keep growing, eventually that same leader goes from being the one "making it happen" to the one "getting in the way." Thus, the more important leadership skills become knowing how to steer the ship, empower others, and then get out of the way. Leadership development, organizing principles, and rich traditions become especially important if you want your community to transcend the limits of a particular leader's personality and continue to grow long after you're gone.

YOU CAN'T DO IT ALONE

You need your team. While it's tempting to go it alone when your team is slowing you down, and it may be true that you could get it done better and faster (this time) doing it yourself, it's important to take the long view. We can get little wins by ourselves, but big wins require others. It takes our team and our tribe.

Take the time to build personal relationships with your leadership team and key volunteers. Put in the effort to build some consensus and get people fully enrolled in the vision so they can help you charge forward with it. Leave room for each person on your team to be the hero. Learn to make everyone around you better. Communicate that they are needed and that you believe they have what it takes. Create a culture of accountability, teamwork, loving your people, and communicating the big vision. Then go build something meaningful together.

REFLECT

- Are you guilty of sending information more frequently than you've earned?

- Poll your team: How enrolled is your flock? (Grade yourself from 1–10.)

- Are you operating in a way that will eventually lead to a raging fire of a ministry? How can you better prioritize intensity over scale?

- What are you doing today to develop the leaders and processes you will need tomorrow?

CHAPTER TEN

Don't Assume They Know

You've said it a hundred times. I get it. But when it comes to your goals and big vision as a leader, you're probably still not saying it enough. Of course, you know all about it. And, yes, your closest circle is tired of hearing about it all. But most of your flock? They have little to no idea yet. Even your most engaged folks need to hear it more before fully absorbing and internalizing it.

Many leaders get trapped in a bubble of their most engaged people. Once they sense their friends and inner circle have gotten the message, they ease up and stop talking about it as much, not wanting to be tiresome or boring or repetitive to them. This is a mistake, and it is one reason we so often only engage the people who are already engaged. If you want the outer circle to eventually get it, keep communicating.

Remember, you and your coworkers think about this stuff all day (and perhaps for many, many years now). For the average person in the pew, they've maybe heard somebody announce it once at the same time their toddler was "whispering" in their ear,

"Have I be'd good enough for a donut today?" Andy Stanley, in his book *Visioneering*, says you need to discuss the vision twenty-one times before it really sinks in. Then you still have to restate it continually after that (in varied, creative ways) so everything else you do stays rooted in that vision.

So don't assume your flock knows the big vision or the reason you exist. They probably don't yet, especially not to the point of internalizing it. Likewise, don't assume they really know what your church is offering them to get involved with just because it's on the website and in the bulletin and has been announced a couple times. Don't presume they even think those things are important at all yet. We take it for granted because we live and breathe it. They aren't there yet.

RIGHT UNDER THEIR NOSES

Let's recall what really motivates people to get involved and follow:

- Something big at stake (ultimate meaning)
- Opportunities for personal growth
- To be needed (responsibility)
- To be truly seen and known
- To believe that tomorrow can be better than today (hope)
- Finding something worth sacrificing everything for (love)

- A stable, safe tribe to do it all with
- Having leaders they trust and believe can help achieve all these things

Your church has the potential to check every single box and do so better than anything else in the world (along with the family). Don't assume the average person already knows this—they don't. They're out there searching for these things elsewhere, looking right past your church in the process. Thus, many people end up leaving without really knowing what they're leaving. There are many challenges to helping our message break through, but it starts with at least making sure we are telling (and repeatedly reminding) them of these basic things in the first place. Don't assume they already know.

They may not know that God is speaking to them right now—in Scripture and prayer, yes, but also through the circumstances of their lives. Through their limits. In their trials. Through their gifts and desires. Through the needs of those around them. Through the natural law. Through all of creation. Through the people God has placed uniquely into their lives.

They may not know that the greatest adventures are not travel to exotic places, achievement of more honors, or the novelty of new things, but rather in quietly going deep into the relationships already in front of them. That in the mysteries of their marriage, the miracle of a child, the needs of a next-door neighbor, God has already given them people to protect, dragons to slay, and the opportunity to love dangerously, vulnerably, and completely.

They may not know the fulfillment, joy, and peace that comes from service—feeding the hungry, visiting the imprisoned, and comforting the sorrowful. Nor the freedom that comes from forgiveness, the humility from humiliation, the great value of suffering, the joy of a good death.

They may not know who they are and the Great Story they are already in. Nor that the demands of the Christian life, though costly, are worth it. And the even better news, that this tremendous burden becomes easy and light when we yoke ourselves to Jesus.

Don't be shy about reminding them. They need it. We all need it. Help your people rediscover these kinds of treasures—already sitting right under their noses—and they'll follow you anywhere. Right now, they don't know what they are leaving. Remind them until they do.

REPEATING YOURSELF WITHOUT BEING ANNOYING

Does this mean we just keep sending more and more emails and repeating ourselves (twenty-one times) over and over until the message gets through? Definitely not. If you do that, people will get bored and annoyed and tune you out (and so will hear it zero times).

So what do we do? When it comes to your overall vision, you must patiently and creatively find new ways of weaving pieces of it into everything you do. Don't tire of repeating yourself, but keep it fresh by learning how to say the same thing in different ways (mentioning it at different events, from different angles, via different mediums, in different contexts, and at varying depths). And make a habit of connecting every little thing you do—whether fixing the toilets, starting a new program, or building a cathedral—to how it fits into that bigger vision.

And remember, it's not just the big *vision* people need to hear over and over. It's anything important. Let's say we have a program starting this fall that we'd like every married couple to participate in. How do we repeat ourselves over and over so everyone knows about it without being annoying?

First, as previously mentioned, you have to earn the right to repeat yourself by doing something they care enough about and communicating it in a clear, direct, convincing way.

Second, announce it like you mean it. If you believe it will be good for people, act like it. Fully commit. You shouldn't be indifferent about whether people attend or not. Let people see how much you care that they come. Make a big deal and focus on it. Don't just copy and paste it into some corner of the bulletin or lump it in with ten other announcements (which often haven't earned the right to be repeated anyway).

Finally, find ways to creatively repeat the message in different ways. Unfortunately, how this usually goes is we write a paragraph of text about our event, then we read it word for word from the pulpit and also copy and paste the same exact text into the bulletin.

Then we repeat that for four weeks in a row. That's not a good way to do it. Instead, let's consider, for example, our marriage program starting this fall. Here's how it could go instead. Initial promotion:

- A direct announcement on Sunday
- A focused email
- A dedicated flyer
- A full page (or front cover) spread in the bulletin (Each customized for the medium)

Then it gets repeated:

- As a *secondary* mention in the next weekly email
- As a quick reminder announcement next Sunday to reserve your spot
- As a reminder on the way out ("Pick up a flyer if you haven't gotten one yet!")

Then you get creative:

- Email out a one-minute video testimonial of how somebody's life changed after attending last year.
- Somewhere else, share a beautiful reflection on marriage in general (not about the program, but with a link/mention at the end to check out the program).

- That same Sunday, during Sunday school, have the children draw a picture of their family to give to their parents.
- Another week, work in a joke about marriage on Sunday morning related to the readings that day (with an encouragement at the end for married couples to sign up).
- Invite a married couple to get up and share why they are attending this year.
- Ask some ministries (that tend to have married people involved) to share it at their next meeting.
- On another Sunday, hand out a free pamphlet or book on the importance of marriage (putting the program flyer inside).
- Invite everyone to a family movie night to celebrate the program kick-off. Watch *Sleeping Beauty* (the original, of course).

And you also recruit help:

- All those already engaged people who've been listening to everything so far and are now getting tired of you talking about it all the time? Recruit them to join the mission. Ask them to personally invite three married couples they know.
- Set a goal for attendance. Tell people about the goal. Ask them to help you reach it.

- Have some volunteers mingle with the crowd on Sunday morning, asking people if they know about the event and whether they plan to attend.
- Email those who have already signed up and see if they'll ask just one friend if they are also attending.
- Get a team of helpers to personally call up every married couple in the community who hasn't signed up yet and let them know they are invited and we'd love to have them.

That is how you repeat yourself without becoming monotonous and, if done well, not annoying either. And by the end, you'll be sure people not only know about it but also know how important it is to you and how much you'd love to see them there. All important things to communicate.

REFLECT

- Think back through your spiritual journey. What is something you didn't know when you were younger (that you probably take for granted now) that you wish people would have told you then?

- What upcoming event or program (just pick one) could you prioritize this year and creatively *repeat* the invitation for?

CHAPTER ELEVEN

How to Get Their Attention

It's the scarcest thing in the world today, and you're giving it to me right now. What is it? Attention.

Herbert Simon points out that "what information consumes is rather obvious: it consumes the attention of its recipients. Hence a wealth of information creates a poverty of attention and a need to allocate that attention efficiently among the overabundance of information sources that might consume it."

That means that once we have somebody's attention, even just for a moment, we better make the most of it. But how do we get their attention in the first place? Especially in an increasingly competitive and noisy landscape and with the overabundance of information in the world today? Here are five strategies:

1. BY INTERSECTION

So you're chatting with a friend about how you'd really like to slow down in life, relax more, and take more naps. You both agree that getting a cat that lounges around the house all day, constantly on the prowl for a new cozy spot to snooze, might inspire you to relax more. You also think a Winnie the Pooh beanbag chair could do the same and would be less moody. But you're still leaning toward the cat.

Well, later that day you're surfing the internet and you all of a sudden notice cat food ads popping up. How did they know?! Our first suspicion is that Big Tech must have been listening in on my conversation and is now trying to sell me stuff! And as much as that may happen sometimes, there is often another dynamic at play.

We are bombarded with literally thousands of advertisements per day and billions of bits of information. But our brains have learned to ignore almost all of it. This is a primitive survival technique. We are wired this way. Our brains are trained to notice new and unusual things (like predators, enemies, danger, or opportunity) and also things that we desperately need (like food or a mate). Our spidey-senses are finely tuned to see the things we (think we) need to notice. Most everything else we've learned to tune out. In other words, it may be that the cat food ads were there all along but now your brain was tuned in to notice. *People hear what they need.*

So how can our message stand out amidst so much noise and competing messages? Answer: Start with something the person is already looking for (something they need) rather than what you want them to know. If our communications are answering questions people haven't even asked, on topics they aren't yet interested in, why should we be surprised that they don't pay attention? They will ignore most anything they aren't already looking for. Instead, start with where your goals and mission intersect with their self-perceived needs.

They may not have a particular passion (yet) for helping the needy one thousand miles away, but maybe that's because they are up to their eyeballs in their own debt and stressed about how to make their mortgage payment next week. They're not interested in visiting the sick or imprisoned across town because their spouse just left them and they feel alone and depressed. They won't respond to an invitation to lead a small group because they don't yet see themselves as worthy or capable of doing so.

People are struggling with everyday life stuff: finances, relationships, self-image, suffering in the world, fears, anxiety. That's what's on their mind, so they are more likely to notice something that speaks to that. Start there as a way in. (Just don't get stuck there.)

One of the most influential communicators of the twentieth century, Archbishop Fulton Sheen (whose 1950s TV show reached thirty million people a week), would start a show on something relevant, timely, and interesting to people, like communism, teen-agers, why work is boring, laughter, loneliness, babies, neuroticism, getting drunk, suffering, the sexual revolution, or how to think. And he'd end up teaching about the Christian faith. Start with what's on their mind. What are they currently debating online or with their friends and family? Start with the questions they are currently asking. Yes, that means you sometimes have to wade into politics and hot-button social issues—of course! The idea that we shouldn't is making us boring and irrelevant. Take courage; be not afraid. Tackle something relevant to them and see what happens.

2. BY DISARMING THEM

When you can assume that your audience holds the same beliefs you do, you can relax and use more normal means of talking to it; when you have to assume that it does not, then you have to make your vision apparent by shock—to the hard of hearing you shout, and for the almost-blind you draw large and startling figures.

—Flannery O'Connor

There are many ways to "shout" or "draw large and startling figures." But the goal is the same: To get their attention and then catch them with their guard down. Then maybe, just maybe, the message strikes them from a new angle or fresh perspective that finally sinks in.

Uniqueness and novelty generally work well, but only if used sparingly. Use them, but know that the newness wears off quickly. The same goes for surprising and shocking people (the next time always needing to be more shocking than the last). But there are other ways to startle and disarm them, like laughter, beauty, goodness, and appeals to the heart. These never get old.

Laughter is one of the best. It can, as Bishop Barron has observed, "turn the soil of the heart and make it more receptive to the planting of the Gospel seed." Science has continually affirmed the power of laughter as medicine. One article by medical experts notes that "laughter strengthens your immune system, boosts mood, diminishes pain, and protects you from the damaging effects of stress. Nothing works faster or more dependably to bring your mind and body back into balance than a good laugh. Humor lightens your burdens, inspires hope, connects you to others, and keeps you grounded, focused, and alert. It also helps you release anger and forgive sooner."

Beauty is irresistible and always leads us to truth and goodness (since they are all deeply connected). That's why Dostoevsky said beauty will save the world. It arrests the heart, boggles the mind, and takes our breath away. Beautiful things are not just to look at but to look through. They are windows to heaven—"doors in the walls of the world"—through which our souls experience God. Do not underestimate the disarming and evangelizing power of simply looking at something beautiful. Create beautiful experiences. Build beautiful spaces. Do beautiful work.

Goodness works well too. Sometimes I am pessimistic about the way the world is going. Then I see my son help his sister tidy up the mess their baby brother made in the living room, all giggling as they work. Immediately I can't remember what I was so pessimistic about only moments before. (Have you ever heard a baby that can't stop laughing?) Nobody had to explain anything to me. No problems in the world were solved. I simply witnessed something good. When your message doesn't seem to be getting through, don't overthink it. Just do something good.

Finally, as previously mentioned, we are emotional creatures. Don't speak with spreadsheets and monotonous facts; speak by showing faces of people you know. Speak creatively and visually. Speak in a way that ignites the imagination. The intellect alone rarely moves people into action; rather, as St. John Henry Newman explains, it's their hopes and fears, likes and dislikes, appetites, passions, and affections that help move them to action. Appeal to their hearts as well as their minds. Engage the imagination to do so.

Anaïs Nin said, "It is the function of art to renew our perception. What we are familiar with we cease to see. The writer shakes up the familiar scene, and, as if by magic, we see a new meaning in it." We need to shake up the familiar scenes our flocks have long tuned out, presenting the ordinary as fresh and new, catching them off guard, and helping them see what is really there. We need another renaissance of beautiful art and of more artful ways of communicating.

3. BY PERSONAL FRIENDSHIP

Most marketing tactics in the world are designed to be used on strangers. (That's why they are often terrible advice for ministry.)

They spend billions of dollars, develop the most advanced technologies, and enlist the most creative minds just to figure out how to get something precious from you that you are already giving to your friends every day for free: your attention.

Friendship earns you second chances, the right to be heard, and the benefit of the doubt. A friend is a trusted source. A friend is willing to see it from your perspective. What a friend says (and does) communicates libraries more than any soundbite, video, blog post, or viral image ever could. If they aren't engaging or listening to what you have to say, consider just being friends first (with no agenda or ulterior motives). How you do friendship can speak far more about God than any words you ever say.

4. BY REMOVING BARRIERS

"Noise is the music of hell."
—C.S. Lewis, *Screwtape Letters*

As Matthew Kelly notes, engaged members of their church (1) study their faith, (2) pray regularly, (3) are generous with their time and treasure serving others, and (4) can't help but share their faith with the world (evangelize). So, naturally, what does the devil do? He makes their heads too tired to study, their lives too noisy to pray, their schedules too busy for others, and their spirits too anxious to evangelize.

People are naturally drawn to God. We are made for him. He is the only thing that finally satisfies. So why aren't people running toward him? Because barriers keep them from seeing clearly.

Perhaps one of the most effective ways to help the message break through is not by addition but by subtraction. Help people clear away the distraction and noise from their lives so they can see clearly. Give them silence, not noise. Help them do less, not more.

5. BY LOVE

In the very early Church, Christians were known by their love. It wasn't that they were friendly and nice to everyone; it's that they selflessly served others in radical, shocking ways. At a time when malformed infants, the mentally disabled, and the seriously ill were cast out or left to die alone, Christians cared for them, even when they were outsiders or enemies. They turned the other cheek. Rather than seek revenge, Christians forgave those who persecuted them. Their love was so radical that it stood out as peculiar and extraordinary. Anyone who encountered it was struck by something sublime and strange, compelling them to consider a new way of looking at the world.

Love is always the way in. It is, in fact, the perfection of every other way in. Love shocks and disarms, it removes barriers, it builds friendship, and people always need it.

Shock people by how much you care and by what you are willing to sacrifice (your whole life) to live out your faith and do what is right. Shock them with your radical concern for ultimate ends, revealing the triviality of so many of our priorities. Shock them with the bigness of your vision. Shock them with how much God forgives them by forgiving them over and over and over. Shock them with how much you love not just your friends but your enemies too. Do that and you'll have their attention.

Remember, God's way of getting our attention was not to conquer Rome by force or to launch a marketing campaign but to wait for thousands of years and then quietly sneak behind enemy lines as an unsuspecting baby in a manger and let us nail him to a cross. He was willing to be patient, to make the sacrifices, to get creative, and to take the long way around. So must we.

CHALLENGE

- For each of the five strategies, write down one way you could apply the strategy to a particular project this year.

CHAPTER TWELVE

Say Different Things to Different People

Would you love to see your email open rate go from 32% to 58%? That's exactly what the communication coordinator, Raymond Figueroa, did at St. Joan of Arc Catholic Church. What was the key? Being purposeful about their messaging and segmenting their communications to make sure the right groups got the right messages.

32% is actually a good open rate for emails sent to large groups (and still way better than just about every other channel you might use aside from text messaging). But it is not uncommon for churches—like Raymond's—to regularly get 50–60% or higher open rates once they implement some important best practices. One of the most important lessons is learning to say different things to different people.

DON'T SAY EVERYTHING TO EVERYONE

First, if your message is for everyone, then it's really for no one in particular. That alone causes people to automatically tune it out. Second, usually most of what's being said isn't actually for everyone. Only one smaller group within the audience really needs to hear it. This dynamic is why many people have tuned out 100% of Sunday announcements and rarely read the bulletin. Practically speaking, most of the information is simply not for them. If I regularly find that only 5% of the information in a given communication is for me, I build the habit of ignoring 100% of it. It's rarely worth the effort of sorting through the other 95% of it just to find the information for me. So that's the first rule: Don't say everything to everyone. And whatever you do say to everyone, make sure that it is truly relevant to a large majority of the people listening.

DIFFERENT WAYS TO SEGMENT YOUR COMMUNICATIONS

There are many ways to segment your communications (i.e., to send different things to different people). The most obvious and practical way is by what people are already involved in. If only a particular ministry or group needs to get a message, then only send it to that group (rather than to everyone). For instance, if only the hospitality ministry needs to hear something, don't send it to everyone or announce it to everyone on Sunday. Just send it to those involved in the hospitality ministry. Pretty straightforward, but you'd be surprised how many churches make this mistake every week.

Next, sometimes you need to segment by various demographic data. For example, an event for kids doesn't need to be promoted over and over again to everyone. Instead, target the adults who have kids. Same with the upcoming marriage retreat: target those who are married.

Finally, perhaps the most powerful way to segment is doing so by levels of engagement. One of the most egregious mistakes I see churches make is when asking for money. They send the same message to everyone—whether it's their first Sunday in ten years, they haven't missed a Sunday in ten years, or (tragically) they haven't shown up for ten years. It's not only ineffective communication, but it can also be harmful to the relationships we're trying to build.

Your relationship with each group is different. Each group is ready for different next steps. Each group is in a different place and has different needs and interests. Different channels and forms of communication work better with different groups. Our messaging strategy must reflect that and be able to differentiate accordingly.

One high-level way to differentiate levels of engagement is the following: the 7%, the 11%, and the 82%. It's overly simple, but that's what makes it so helpful.

These numbers happen to be based upon consistent research done on established Catholic parishes, but the same concept applies regardless of denomination. The exact percentages will of course vary based upon the phase of life your church community is in (especially if it's relatively new and will by default have a higher proportion of engaged people). But I believe all communities tend toward similar numbers over time, and, regardless, the lessons remain the same. (These numbers are also currently trending in the wrong direction and so are likely even worse by the time you're reading this.)

THE 7%

The 7% are the ones who do almost all (about 90%) of the financial giving and volunteering. The 7% are, for the most part, "in." They've stuck with us through any hard times and are fully committed to the community no matter what. They are relatively easy to communicate with. They read the bulletin, listen to announcements, check the website, show up multiple times per week, read your emails, and may even download your app or follow you on social media.

THE 11%

The 11% are at the other end of the spectrum. This is the percentage of folks who don't show up at all anymore (but still identify as part of your community). While they still need to be evangelized, they are much harder to reach since we no longer have an active relationship with them (though we may still be able to reach them if we get an email address or phone number from them when we have the chance).

THE 82%

In between the two extremes of the 7% (most engaged) and the 11% (not engaged), you have what I call the 82%. These folks are still showing up . . . sometimes.

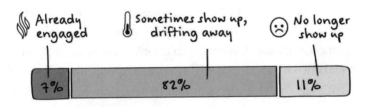

Some of them (14% out of the 82%) are actually there in the pews faithfully every Sunday. (They just aren't volunteering or donating much.) The rest of the 82% (the vast majority) attend less frequently and more sporadically—that is, every other week, monthly, once in a blue moon, or only Christmas and Easter.

Right now, most of the 82% are drifting further out of the Church. The good news (and the key reason why the 82% is where our main focus should be) is that they are still sitting there in front of us, in person, giving us attention, participating at some level, at least some Sundays each year. We must engage them before it's too late. That starts with naming them, being more deliberate in our communications toward them, and understanding that they are different than the 7%.

WHY WE STRUGGLE TO ENGAGE THE DISENGAGED

Church leaders usually have good intentions of reaching the 82%, but in practice, the study programs, questions answered, activities offered, and language used tend to only resonate with the 7%—not the 82%. Likewise, the software, content, and communication tools that many assume work best (mobile apps, social media channels, high-touch software solutions, etc.) mostly only work in real life with an already highly engaged group, like the 7%.

Why do church leaders continue to struggle to engage the 82%? Because the folks making these decisions are typically among the 7% themselves. Most complaints, praises, comments, reactions, impressions, and other feedback come from the 7%. Most of the money donated comes from the 7%. It's all happening within "the 7% bubble." So it's only natural for leaders to see everything through that lens, but it's a key reason why we still struggle to engage those who are slowly drifting away (the 82%).

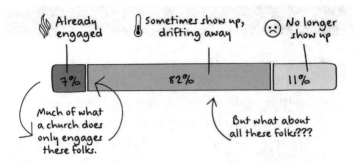

To be successful, we must break out of that 7% feedback loop, acknowledge that much of what we do now is done by and for the 7%, get intentional about precisely who we are trying to reach, and be willing to try a different approach, saying different things to different people.

SELF-ASSESSMENT

- Examine your announcements, bulletin, and weekly email newsletter from last week. Is there anything in there that doesn't need to be said to everyone? How could you send only that part directly to the folks who need to hear it?

- Is your church currently equipped with the right tools? Can you segment your messaging by ministry involvement, demographic, or various levels of engagement (using a tool like Flocknote or something similar)?

CHAPTER THIRTEEN

Did You Miss Me?

"Sometimes we sit next to people for years and don't know who they are," explained Kathy McCleary, Communication and Volunteer Coordinator at St. Pius X Parish. To fix that, she helped implement "Name Tag Weekend," where people stuck on a simple name tag when they walked in that Sunday. "Everyone had so much fun with it!" she shared. And it made it easy to finally reengage that person who's been sitting next to you in the same pew for five years—when you should really already know their name, but you're only 80% sure what it is, so you just don't say anything, and now it's been so long it's embarrassing to ask again.

This seems like a small thing, but it strikes deeply at what may be the most important lesson in this book. Does your flock know your voice? Can you call them by name? Does anyone even know their name? Do you really know your flock? What is your relationship with them? And what is their relationship with each other?

It's easy to think of big meaningful things meaning large crowds or lots of people knowing about it. But that's not what makes something "big." What makes it big is the extent to which it impacts the soul of an individual person. It's personal. It may be a small, trivial thing to everyone else, but it's big to them.

Dale Carnegie said, "A person's name is to that person the sweetest and most important sound in any language." When a person hears their name, it literally causes a rush of positive hormones in their brain. It's one way we say to a person, "I see you" (not just that I see any ol' person, but that I see *you*). But why does it have this effect? Because we are wired to be seen and known—to be loved.

In the Zulu tribe from Southern Africa, the most common greeting they use doesn't have a direct English equivalent. Instead of a simple "Hello" or "How are you?" they say "Sawubona," which translates to something like "I see you." They don't just mean "I see you standing there," but "I recognize your full humanity and everything that makes up who you are, where you've been, what's on your heart." I see you.

So yes, know their name, but know it because you truly see them, know them, love them, and miss them when they're gone.

THE TEST

If you have one hundred people in your group and one stops showing up, do you notice that person is missing? And if so, what do you do about it?

In some ways, this could be considered *the* question for a ministry leader. It is one of our essential tasks: to miss people and do something about it. "Which one of you, having a hundred sheep and losing one of them, does not leave the ninety-nine in the wilderness and go after the one that is lost until he finds it?" (Luke 15:4).

The good shepherd leaves the group to find the one (Uno, remember?). What if that's what we did with the groups we lead? How many people would still be drifting out of them? What do we do when one of our people goes missing? Do we even notice? How long does it take for us to notice? There are few things more impactful to a relationship than being missed—when your absence is noticed and felt by somebody.

Think about a time you weren't able to participate in an event or gathering and the next time somebody saw you they went out of their way to ask, "Hey, I noticed you weren't at the BBQ last Sunday? You were missed." Or maybe they proactively reached out to you before even seeing you next with a text or a phone call and asked where you were. That's even more powerful.

Now flip it around. Think of a time you had to miss something and afterward nobody said anything. Nobody noticed you weren't there. Nobody missed you. It's deflating and sobering for any relationship.

How often does somebody miss a Sunday Mass or event at your church without anyone noticing? Did anyone miss them?

What about after they miss multiple Sundays? Or don't show up for months? Does anyone miss them?

If somebody is new to a group or lurking in the periphery, they are constantly, even if only subconsciously, asking themselves, "Does it matter to these people if I'm here?" This may be the single biggest factor that determines whether somebody comes back, even more than other more rational reasons, like whether they enjoy it or whether it's good for them. Do these people care if I'm here?

People know when nobody misses them; they can feel it. And that, often more than anything we say, communicates a powerful message they hear loud and clear: "We don't care if you show up. You don't really matter to our community."

Just like the shepherd going after Uno, it's not rocket science. It doesn't require creativity, money, or great skill. You just have to do it. Here's a few tips:

1. Preemptively make sure you're communicating that they will be missed if they don't come. You can communicate this to everyone at once, but that is not very effective. It needs to be personal (go after the one). "Do you plan to come next week? I'd love to see you."

2. Notice. Just like a good shepherd, any time you gather, take note of who is there and who is missing. It can be a quick mental note in small groups, or it might mean quietly taking attendance in larger groups. You may even need a volunteer to help you.

3. Follow up (i.e., go after them!). It doesn't have to be some grand effort. Even the simplest of gestures sends one of the most powerful messages: I thought of you. Next time you see them, say, "Hey, we missed you last week!" Even better, don't wait until you see them again. (Show them you were thinking of them without needing the reminder of seeing them again first.) Reach out *before* you see them again and it will be even more powerful.

4. Create a culture of missing your people (i.e., a culture of going after the one that is lost). Set the example with your own leadership, but then train up your leaders and other influential people to do the same. In large groups, one person can't have a personal relationship with everyone. You won't be able to miss everyone by yourself. But you can build an environment where everyone is missed by at least somebody and everyone has at least one friend to *go after them* if they don't show up.

REFLECT

- What is one thing you could do to miss your people better?

- What can you do to make sure you (as a team) can call each one of your flock by name?

CHAPTER FOURTEEN

The Best Communication Channels

It was super awkward. I had just done multiple conference pre-sentations on church communication, particularly on the use of email, and it was time for the Q&A session (my favorite part). And this lady stands up, in front of hundreds of other church leaders, and says, "Come on . . . why are we talking about email? Nobody reads email anymore."

The awkward part was not her question but figuring out how to say (in much gentler words) that it's not that people don't read email anymore; it's that they don't read her email anymore.

People read more email today than ever before in history. We just receive a lot more too. And we've become really efficient at scanning through it to read the email we care about most (and ignoring the rest). But it raises the question: What are the most effective communication channels today? And where should a church put most of its energy to get the best results?

After years and years at Flocknote, helping churches improve communication and exploring many different communication technologies in the process, we continually kept coming back to two channels that stood head and shoulders above the rest. In terms of getting real results and leading the flock, *email and text messaging* did it better and more consistently than anything else. Here are a few reasons why.

THE NEW HOME ADDRESS

It used to be that having the physical "home address" (i.e., mailing address) where somebody lived was the most important thing to collect. This used to be the contact info that changed the least and where you could reach them years from now if you ever needed to. This is not the case any longer. Nowadays, people change mobile phone numbers and email addresses even less than their physical mailing addresses.

It's easy to understand why. First, their email address and mobile phone is how people communicate with and access the most important people (family, friends, coworkers) and institutions (banks, social networks, bills, etc.) in their lives. We rely on our mobile number and email address more than any other communication channels. And, while we used to change these fairly often, the average person now tends to keep the same email address and mobile phone number for much of their lives. They are the new "home addresses" for your members.

BEST OPEN RATES

The "open rate" is, generically speaking, the percentage of people who actually end up opening and reading a particular message you send. This is helpful in assessing effectiveness and how much time is worth investing in each of these channels.

Channel	Open Rate	
The bulletin	5%	(based upon my personal polling of thousands of church leaders)
Facebook	6%	(percentage of your followers that see a given post—unless you pay extra)
Mobile app	7–15%	(number of folks who will bother to download the app and keep notifications on—generally the same folks you're already reaching other ways)
Email	25–60%+	(largely depends on quality of email and leadership)
Text messaging	99%	(with 97% read within fifteen minutes of sending)

Edie Brewer had a problem. Every year, St. Bartholomew's Parish participated in the town's annual German Sausage Festival. But one year, just before the event, they realized they were eight hundred kiefels short, and time was running out. Edie, a volunteer leader, pulled up Flocknote on her phone and immediately sent out the following text message to the group: "SOS: If you have a rolling pin and some time, please ride over to the Parish Hall at St. Barts right now. They are short on help and have 800 more kiefels to make. Thank you!" Immediately, additional volunteers showed up, and the keifel shortage was averted. (The next week they sent out an email newsletter sharing pictures of all the baking and other efforts that made it possible.)

At the height of the pandemic, Tina Gregory (Communications Coordinator at St. Michael's) helped her parish start a volunteer-supported drive-thru food pantry that now serves about one thousand people each Saturday. They use Flocknote's Signups feature to manage volunteer slots and send text messages to remind people about their assignments. Any time they need a substitute or some extra help, they just text message the group. She says, "Our response time is maybe two minutes. It's incredible!"

Sophia Bauer, Communications Specialist at St. Thomas More University Parish, explained how they started off trying to reach their students "spending thousands on an app, but nobody was enabling push notifications, nobody was interacting with it." So instead they switched to email and text messaging, using Flocknote, and immediately started reaching way more people and getting far more engagement. They used it to transition to an electronic bulletin, which is more engaging and interactive, and regularly text students reminders for scheduled events or with room or time changes. Sophia says, "People are able to engage with us a lot more, and it's easy because there is nothing they have to download, no extra steps; they just reply back." It just works.

REACHING PEOPLE YOU'RE NOT YET REACHING

It's helpful to step back and clarify the problem we're trying to solve. The challenge is usually not "How do we reach our most engaged folks?" Those folks are engaged enough to get the message whichever way we send it. And they make up the bulk of the people who are already paying attention and who may download your app, follow you on Facebook, and read the bulletin. The more important question is: "Which channels are most likely to reach everybody else, particularly the folks who are less engaged and/ or drifting away?" (The 82%, remember?) In that case, texting and email become even more preferred.

This is largely because, with email and texting, people don't have to create an account, download an app, log in somewhere, or otherwise do anything to receive information from you. They are already checking their emails and text messages all day long. If we send high-quality communications, these channels have the best chance of breaking through. Replying back is also easy for them, allowing additional personal conversations to naturally occur as a result.

EVERYTHING ELSE GETS EASIER

Once you have a member's email and/or mobile phone number (and a solid way to use them), everything else you need to do gets much easier. Not only can you now reach everyone with an urgent reminder or sudden change of schedule, but if you need more info from them, you can reach them directly and invite them to take a next step, click a link, donate, RSVP, answer your question, visit your website, fill out a form, give you more info, or otherwise respond to some call to action you have for them.

At Flocknote we call this a "communications-first" approach. Every church should start with being able to effectively communicate with and directly reach each person. Once you can do that, managing member info, raising money, getting volunteers, or otherwise getting people to engage and join the mission is way more successful. All of our software is designed with that in mind. Most other church software evolved from a different starting point (database, online payments, etc.) and then added on communication features later. Communicating is the core of what we do rather than an add-on, and, as a result, it allows us to fulfill so many other church software needs in uniquely effective ways.

SAFEST, SUREST, AND
LEAST LIKELY TO GET CENSORED

In the end, if you're going to go through all this work to build up a way of communicating with your flock, it is wise to invest in direct channels that are also platform-independent. In that regard, there is nothing better than email and text messaging.

If you have a person's email address and cell phone number, you can use them on any number of different tools and platforms. There is no Big Tech company in the middle—controlling the channel, tool, social network, or app store—who may decide to censor you or get in the way. You can take email addresses and cell phone numbers and use them in any other tool and always be able to directly reach your people.

For all of these reasons and more, there are no other communication channels anywhere near as valuable as email and text messaging. None. Now, you might be thinking I'm biased toward email and text messaging because Flocknote specializes in them. But it's actually the other way around. The very reason Flocknote built all of our services (communication, signups, online payments, member management, and much more!) around a sophisticated way to email and text message your flock is precisely because we spent more than a decade learning each of these lessons the hard way. (In fact, before Flocknote, I spent years building a totally different church communication tool that failed because I hadn't learned these lessons yet.) For a church, there is simply no better communication ROI (return on investment) than prioritizing email and text messaging.

REFLECT

- Take inventory: write down all the various communication channels your church (and all of its ministries) is currently using.

- If you could only choose four of them, which would you keep? Why?

CHAPTER FIFTEEN

Say Less, Communicate More

"I'm sorry I wrote you such a long letter. I didn't have time to write you a short one."

—Blaise Pascal

In a crisis of communication, where our message clearly isn't getting through, our natural instinct is to go out and say more. But this can do, and often does, more harm than good—particularly in an increasingly competitive and noisy media environment.

It's a lot harder to say what you want to say in a short letter than in a long one. You have to be more thoughtful. You have to decide what's important and what isn't. It takes more of your time and energy. But whether it's the words on your website, in your bulletin, in a speech, or in an email, the length communicates a lot. And it could be the key factor as to whether or not somebody reads it.

A short letter says to the recipient: "I care about and respect your time. I've bothered to be thoughtful by taking my own time to be decisive and, rather than saying everything, have chosen the most important things I want you to know—and I've left the rest out."

People are distracted and bombarded with information all day long. They have little time for long letters and even less patience for those who are careless with their time. Right now many organizations say quite a lot, but they communicate very little (because nobody reads it). Instead, say less and you'll communicate more.

When you hand out your Sunday bulletin (which has undoubtedly grown longer and longer over the years), what percentage of your flock receives a particular message you put inside it? The average answer (after personally asking thousands of church leaders) is that 5% of their flock get the message (and many are not even that optimistic!). But the point is, most people don't really read the long-form bulletin. Now, consider if instead of your bulletin this Sunday you handed out a single piece of paper with four quick bullet points on the front—the four most important things you want your flock to know this week. What percentage of them would know those four things? Almost all of them! You'll have said a lot less, but you'll have communicated a lot more.

I'm not saying we need to be that extreme in rethinking the bulletin, but it illustrates the point nicely. Take the extra time to write somebody a short letter rather than a long one (no matter what the channel). It's worth your time and effort. Such brevity is not only the soul of wit but the goal of your writ.

BAD HABITS FROM SCHOOL

In school we'd often get graded based upon how many pages (12 pt., double-spaced) we turned in. This trained us to be bad writers, rewarding the filling up of space rather than effective communication. It encouraged us to take something that could be said in one sentence with simple words and to expand it into an entire paragraph of long complex words and fluffy sentences.

A few tips:

- Don't write a page when a paragraph will do.
- Don't use big words when common, familiar words will do.
- Don't use long, complex sentences when short, simple sentences will do.
- Cut out the fluff. Learn to get to the point.
- Making it longer doesn't get you extra points, nor does it communicate that you're smarter or care more. It communicates quite the opposite.

WHAT'S THE LEAD?

In journalism, the "lead" is that short beginning to a news story that attempts to capture the who, what, where, when, and why of the whole story in a concise, clear manner. Nora Ephron, the well-known writer, said her most profound writing lesson came when her Journalism 101 teacher asked the class to write their own lead for a story based on the following facts: "Kenneth L. Peters, the principal of Beverly Hills High School, announced today that the entire high school faculty will travel to Sacramento next Thursday for a colloquium in new teaching methods. Among the speakers will be anthropologist Margaret Mead, college president Dr. Robert Maynard Hutchins, and California governor Edmund 'Pat' Brown."

All the students got to work, constructing their best, most concise "lead" sentence while still including all the facts. Things like "Margaret Mead, Maynard Hutchins, and Governor Brown will address the faculty on . . ." or "Next Thursday the high school faculty will . . ." blah blah blah.

The teacher reviewed their answers and told them they were all wrong. And, in fact, the correct lead to the story was: "There will be no school Thursday."

Immediately, Ephron realized it was not about "regurgitating the facts but about figuring out the point. It wasn't enough to know the who, what, when and where; you had to understand what it meant. And why it mattered."

That's what great communicators are able to do: sort through all the information and capture what is meaningful for your flock. That's what you lead with. That's what gets their attention and motivates them to read further. You can give them all the other details further down or somewhere else. If you're losing their attention or they aren't reading further, it's because your "lead" didn't tap into something that mattered enough to them.

YOU CAN'T NOT COMMUNICATE

While we're on the topic of saying too much, remember that saying nothing at all sends the wrong message too. Silence, the non-response, the awkward pause, the hesitant reply—these are, in fact, powerful ways of communicating. And a church's lack of communication may actually be doing harm. Not communicating may be saying "We don't care" or "I'm scared to lead" or "We just aren't very organized." It may be telling people that we don't think they're important (until we need something from them . . . like money!). Or it could send the message that we must not have anything worth communicating in the first place.

TIMING MATTERS TOO

"Sending one text message at the right time got twice as many people to show up." I've heard this story over and over again. When you remind somebody on Sunday about something happening four days later on Thursday, they say, "Oh yeah, I need to remember to go to that." Then their weekly routine kicks in on Monday and they forget all about it. Instead, try sending a text message reminder the night before, when they are thinking about and planning for the next day. Twice as many people as usual show up.

What's the difference? Timing. Yes, a text message is the most powerful way today to reach a group, period. But when you also get the timing right, the results are tremendous. The same concept applies to any communication channel you're using.

The best thing to do is put yourself in the recipient's shoes. What kind of information are you sending and how? What do you want the person to do as a result of the communication (sign up, reply, give money, etc.)? Then think about when will be the most convenient time of day for this person to receive the message, consume the information, and then (if necessary) take that action.

Here are some examples:

- Let's say you want replies to a question. Rather than texting early Tuesday morning when people are driving to work (and can't immediately reply, and will forget later), wait until they're probably on a lunch break or back home and can reply right away.
- If you want responses to a survey, don't ask during, for example, the Christmas season, when people are focused on and busy with so many other things. Wait until a less busy time.

- If you want them to read something, the worst time may be giving it to them as they're walking toward the parking lot on Sunday, wrangling fussy kids and trying to find a lost shoe. Instead, email it to them later when they're better able to focus on it.

Don't overthink it. For most communications, there are way more important factors than timing. But for some messages, it makes a huge difference.

The key takeaway from this chapter is that if you're willing to put in the extra effort and hone these skills, you can replace numerous poorly timed long letters with one well-timed short letter. You'll say a lot less, but you'll communicate a lot more.

CHALLENGE

Delete 80% of your next message.

- Try cutting out 80% of what you normally want to say (in emails, announcements, etc.), and force yourself to boil it down to the most important 20%. It's hard because the other 80% may be important too. But if everything is important, then nothing is (and readers spend their time accordingly).

- You can still provide links or tell them where they can find the other 80% if they're interested. But you'll find that once it's gone, you don't miss it. What's left will be more elegant, punchy, packed with value, and likely to be read.

- It will take time to see all the fruits of this exercise. You are slowly training your readers/listeners to see that you've done the hard work, reduced it down to what's most valuable, made it quick and easy to consume, and ensured that it's always worth their time.

CHAPTER SIXTEEN

Are You Listening?

Peter Shankman's long, tiring, surprising workday started when his alarm clock went off at 3:30 a.m. He had an early flight to catch from Newark to Tampa, then an entire day of meetings, and then an evening flight that got him back home to his apartment late that night.

The workday, though long, went well. But as he boarded his evening flight home, he realized he hadn't eaten much all day and wouldn't be home until late. He was now very, very hungry. As a steak lover and steakhouse connoisseur, he'd become a fan of the Morton's Steakhouse chain of restaurants. And while waiting for the plane to take off, his mind began to ruminate on steak and his stomach began to rumble, and he impulsively posted on Twitter: "Hey @Mortons – can you meet me at newark airport with a porterhouse when I land in two hours? K, thanks. :)"

He later explained about the tweet, "Let's understand: I was joking. I had absolutely no expectations of anything from that

Tweet. It's like how we Tweet 'Dear Winter, please stop, love Peter,' or something similar."

Next, he turned off his phone, and three hours later he was landing at Newark airport, even hungrier than before. He deplaned and went to find his ride home, who was waiting for him outside the airport pickup area. As he moved to load up his bags, he heard a voice behind him say:

"Uhm, Mr. Shankman. There's a surprise for you here."

He looked up and he saw a man . . . in a tuxedo . . . carrying a Morton's bag!

The man in the tuxedo introduced himself and explained that they had heard he was hungry, and then he handed him the Morton's bag, which contained a "24 oz. Porterhouse steak, an order of Colossal Shrimp, a side of potatoes, one of Morton's famous round things of bread, two napkins, and silverware."

Pretty radical service from Morton's, wasn't it? But isn't that exactly the kind of radical service we are called to in our ministries?

Morton's was listening. Are we listening?

What Morton's did was not herculean—it's dinner for one— but it was radically personal. They were tuned in to the needs of their tribe. They listened and paid attention. And when the opportunity came, they were thoughtful and generous. And in the process, of course, they earned a fan for life, a true follower who has gone on to tell thousands of others just how special Morton's is.

TOO MUCH TALKING

When the topic of communication comes up, and particularly when new technologies are involved, the first thing most of us think about are all the things we want to say and all the new ways we can now say them: "How do we get our message out better? How do we get them to listen to us? How do we use this giant megaphone to our advantage?"

What we sometimes forget to ask is "How can we listen to our people better? What can we do to better understand their needs, their struggles, and what questions they have so we can better serve them?" This is perhaps the greatest need in all relationships today and the key opportunity of the digital age: to be better listeners.

LISTENING WITHOUT CREEPING

I'm not suggesting you need to use the internet to creep on all your people's lives online. And I am certainly not talking about harvesting their information online or benefiting from those who harvest it and sell it. I'm not talking about robots that crawl the internet piecing together data about us that we had no idea was out there, that we wish wasn't out there, and that makes us feel violated and uncomfortable when we find out somebody (like our church!) knows something about us we've never told them.

That may sometimes work for selling products, but it's terrible for building trusting, quality relationships. It's a shortcut that does more harm than good. Instead, go learn from your people by listening to them in ways that don't violate their trust, which is best done from within the natural pursuit of a real, human, personal relationship. Pay better attention to the things they are already telling you in the normal course of a healthy relationship.

BREAKING OUT OF THE ECHO CHAMBER

Some of you may be saying, "Oh trust me, I hear plenty from my flock. I have to listen to unsolicited advice and complaints all day." That may be true, but you're probably hearing disproportionately from a small bubble of people within your community. These tend to be people who are already very engaged, have a close relationship with you, or have a habit of being the squeaky wheel. Listening mostly to them will give you a skewed view of the community's mindsets and needs and make you less able to relate to and reach people outside that bubble.

If you want to know what most of the flock thinks, feels, wants, and needs—especially those who are drifting away and are far less likely to volunteer their thoughts on their own—then be intentional about building relationships with and listening to them.

THE POWER OF ASKING

Sometimes churches sit around trying to guess what their people want, or what they need, or what they'd be excited to do. And they forget to just try asking them! It's amazing what you can learn simply by asking.

You can do this quickly with large groups using a simple pew or email survey (don't make it long, or the less-engaged folks won't participate) or a poll (your email tool should have this kind of feature built in, making it very easy to do). It's also hugely effective to send a quick text message with a short question. Use this sparingly depending on the group, but you get most people's replies within a few minutes. It's amazing. That question you're wondering the answer to? The problem you're trying to solve in your ministry? The answer may be only a few minutes away. Just ask.

And if they aren't responding to your survey or email, don't give up. Don't sit back and say, "They just won't respond." When was the last time you walked up to somebody, politely engaged them in conversation, asked them a question, and then they didn't respond? It doesn't happen very often. Large-scale bulk surveys and polls are extremely efficient and helpful for certain things, but they will never beat one-on-one conversations. And in the hours we spend putting together a survey, designing the email to send it out, and tabulating responses, how many phone calls could we make? How many short conversations could we have on Sunday morning mingling with people? Ten? Twenty? Fifty? Probably. And you'll learn way more that way too.

If your people aren't engaging like you want, just ask them why. It doesn't have to be some mystery problem that you blindly guess at how to fix. Ask the person in the back pew what's on their mind. Then listen. Don't be afraid to ask.

THEIR PAINS AND PROBLEMS

When you spend time listening to your people, you'll not only learn the things they struggle with but hear the precise ways they talk about and describe their struggles. This is really important when searching for synergies and points of intersection between the perceived needs of your people and your mission. You need to understand both what their needs are *and* how they articulate those needs. What words do they use to describe them? What are the root causes of the problems? What kinds of solutions have they already tried that haven't worked?

Then when you attempt to communicate that you can help, you already know and can naturally use the words that make their ears perk up. (Remember, people's brains are naturally tuned to notice things they need.)

They say no one cares how much you know until they know how much you care. It's true. Become a student of your people. Thoughtfully listen and learn what's on their minds. Delight in them—as funny, fascinating creatures made in the image and likeness of God. Slow down and observe. Take an interest in their interests. See what moves them. See when they stop paying attention. Where do they look? When do they smile? How do they respond and to what? Get to know them—not just the collective "them" but each individual. And don't just do it from afar, but jump into their messy lives and go shoulder to shoulder in the pasture, running after the Shepherd together. If you're paying attention, God gives us endless opportunities to serve those around us in radical ways that can change their lives forever.

REFLECT

- How is listening to your flock a core part of your communication strategy?

- What problem are you trying to solve right now that your people may know the answer to? (Why don't you ask them?)

CHAPTER SEVENTEEN

Doing It on Purpose

Wise men speak because they have something to say;
fools because they have to say something.

—Plato

It's easy for a church to fall into a thoughtless habit of communicating without the intentionality it deserves. Maybe it's the boilerplate text on the front of the bulletin, the mechanical reading of some routine part of the announcements, or a sign we let somebody stick on the bulletin board months ago. Or maybe it's a section of the website where we put something, well, because there was an empty place in the website template. Or maybe it was put there a long time ago and we can't remember why, but we keep saying it anyway.

The reason so many church websites are so badly designed is because nobody ever asked, "What's the purpose of this website? What do we want it to achieve?" (and then designed it to do that).

Instead, we just make our website look like other websites we like. That's a recipe for failure.

It's been even worse with the adoption of various social media platforms. We jump on the wagon because everyone says you have to, but we never stop to ask, "What meaningful goal do we want to achieve with this?" It's no wonder we end up spinning our wheels. Once we step back and define the goal, we often realize it simply isn't the right tool for the job or that there are better ways to achieve it.

It's the same for everything we send out. Do we know the goal? Or are we just sending it because we're supposed to send something? Are we just filling up empty space and time, checking a box that says "make a weekly email with news," "send out the schedule," or "post to Facebook daily"... check, check, check?

Zig Ziglar was right: "If you aim at nothing, you will hit it every time." If you have any hope of succeeding, first decide what you're aiming at. Why am I sending this? What is the goal?

GOING THROUGH THE MOTIONS

Sometimes there is, indeed, a good purpose for what we're saying, but we're not saying it on purpose and with purpose. We are just going through the motions. Whenever I visit churches, I often see an example of this when they are welcoming new visitors each Sunday. At some point they usually say something like, "If you're visiting us for the first time, welcome. Please fill out a visitor card so we can keep in touch."

It's a wonderful and important thing to welcome new people. So kudos to you if you're already taking time out to do this. But it is often, as in this example, phrased poorly (not communicating the why, nor saying anything that is convincing, motivating, or inspiring to a visitor). Even worse, it's typically said in a way that sounds like the announcer has made this exact announcement one hundred times before (because they usually have).

It's natural to do this. If your brain has said something one hundred times before, and it also knows you now have to say it again to the same set of mostly familiar faces who have heard it one hundred times before, you get a strong feeling of wanting to skip past it quickly so as not to bore anyone. So you mumble it under your breath hastily and hurry on to the next announcement. But when you do this, visitors can tell that you aren't really talking to them. And it makes it feel as if you don't actually care whether those visitors connect with you or not.

As a leader, this is your chance to acknowledge the presence of new people and welcome them sincerely. (How exciting it is for everyone that there are new people in our midst!) Give compelling reasons why those visitors might want to fill out a visitor card ("to get a weekly update of everything going on" or "to learn more about our mission to do <BLANK>" or "if you'd like to get more involved in X, Y, or Z," etc.). Then announce it like you mean it. Loudly. Confidently. With appropriate pauses and time for people to look and locate the cards before moving to the next thing. Clearly tell them how and what to do, as if you expect that they may actually want to do it. Say it with purpose. Do it on purpose.

GETTING SPECIFIC

Which is more likely to get support?

- Option #1: Help people in Africa.
- Option #2: Help build a basketball court for the 128 young children at a new school in Dodola, Ethiopia, so they can benefit from a proper sports program.

Option #2 gets ten times as much interest and support. Why? Because humans respond much better when the experience is concrete, flesh and bones, and personal. We like specifics, faces, and relationships, and we like to know that something real is at stake. We want to know how we can be a part of a real-life story. People don't respond strongly to vague aspirations ("Save more people" or "Make things better" or "Grow this bigger"). But when abstract things start to have real human consequences, people respond, and our ability to fix problems and make things happen is remarkable. What is typically missing from church leadership is the setting of tangible, motivating goals that clearly communicate what we are trying to achieve and what is at stake.

Consider the following improvements from vague to specific:

Vague	Specific
Give money to our homeless ministry.	Come with us to learn the name of every homeless person in our neighborhood.
Go out and vote your conscience.	Let's get a thousand of us to show up on the steps of the capitol tomorrow and help defeat an unjust law.
Be more selfless in your marriage.	Let's get every single married couple in our community to a marriage retreat this year.
Pray for an end to abortion.	Come pray with us on the sidewalk this weekend, and every week after, until there is nobody left willing to perform an abortion in our town.
Go home and read more Scripture.	Let's do a thirty-day challenge together.
Donate to help our youth program.	Sponsor our Youth Trivia Night (against the adults!) this weekend.
Try to volunteer more.	Help celebrate our patronal feast by choosing a chore to do for our annual day of community service.

The examples are endless. Most churches are already doing inspiring things. They just need to capture the effort more specifically and communicate it a little better. Rather than generically encouraging people to do everything, pick a certain something meaningful to your community instead. Get specific. Set an ambitious but achievable goal, and communicate it. Far more people will enroll in the effort.

A SIMPLE METHOD TO THE MADNESS

"Sometimes I'll start a sentence and I don't even know where it's going. I just hope I find it along the way."
—Michael Scott, *The Office*

Once you've discerned a big goal you'd like to achieve, this simple method will quickly create a solid strategy and plan to help you execute it. You can use this for any kind of goal. It's what Charlene Li and Josh Bernoff call the POST method.

P stands for People. You must begin with who you are trying to reach. As you can imagine, reaching "people in the pews" vs. "strangers on the internet" leads to two very different strategies. So it's important to start here.

Additionally, it's very important during this step to not think about everyone you're trying to reach. Think about one particular person you're trying to reach. Picture them in your head. Now describe them. How old are they? Are they male or female? What are their values? Lifestyle? Challenges in their life? Write down every detail you can about them. For example:

Forty-two-year-old male / father of four young children / works too much / loves Texas Aggie football, early '90s rock, and Wordle / slightly overweight / hits the gym three days in a row every six months

/ in the pew most Sundays but doesn't pray much outside of church / very few close friends who live their faith.

O is for Objective. What would you like to help this person do? How do you want them to be different after they've interacted with you?

Would like him to be a better spiritual leader of his family, who leads them in prayer daily and cultivates an authentically Christian home.

S is for Strategy. What kinds of activities will help you achieve your objective with that person?

Hold a monthly men's washers tournament at the church. Pray together before and after. Each month, give the men a take-home challenge to do one daily prayer activity (pray with your wife before bed, pray with your family at dinner, etc.) and a simple handout with some example prayers to use. Follow up next month to discuss and toss more washers.

T is for technology. Now, after answering all of those other questions, ask: What technologies will help us carry out this Strategy to reach our Objectives with this Person (or group of people)?

We will send an email to the whole group every couple of weeks with reminders, encouragements, an electronic version of the handout, and, of course, the updated tournament standings. And then we'll use text messaging for urgent updates and reminders the night before each event.

The POST method is one of many methods you can use. But regardless of the particular method you choose, there are two main takeaways you mustn't miss:

1. The process should take your mission from something more abstract to something very specific.
2. Notice the order of this method. Many churches fail because they get these backward. They start with the tool or technology ("We know we need this") and then fill in the other categories. It's a recipe for failure. First you must know the People (who you want to reach), Objective (what you want them to do), and Strategy (activities that will achieve that). Only then can you correctly choose which technologies or communication channels will really help you execute.

DON'T MISS THE SECRET INGREDIENT

Failure is not necessarily a bad thing. For a scientist, failure is data. For an optimist, failure is a learning opportunity. For leaders and communicators, failure is just part of the process.

You are going to fail. Any strategy you implement will have some things that work and some things that don't. No big deal.

The thing that many communication strategies are missing is a feedback loop—a time in the not-so-distant future when you assess what is and isn't working and then make adjustments. Too many churches just keep doing the same thing that isn't working. Years go by without change, and guess what? It's still not working.

No process is perfect. So your strategy must have a step built in for measurement, accountability, and adjustments.

A good process must:

1. Begin with deliberate, concrete, measurable goals. Otherwise, there is no way to know in the future if you succeeded or not.
2. Set a time period to measure. Otherwise, you won't know when to check.
3. Assign accountability to one person to lead the project.
4. Include a feedback loop that asks, "Did it work? And if not, why not?" Then adjust and repeat. And don't forget to also ask here, "Was it worth it?" Maybe you met your measurable goal—congrats! But was it worth the cost and effort? Is it helping you achieve your bigger goals and mission in the way you thought it would? Maybe not.

If you have that kind of process, then no matter how bad your strategy starts out, it will always be improving. Eventually, you'll have something that works pretty well.

GETTING THE METRICS RIGHT

It's an amazing phenomenon that what you measure tends to improve. And it's very convenient that so many of our digital tools have the ability to measure all kinds of interesting things. But the important question remains: Which metrics really matter? What exactly should we measure so that it improves?

It can be a trap to simply use the metrics already built-in to the familiar features of the digital landscape—like website traffic, opens, followers, clicks, and likes. There is this assumption that more of all of those must be better. That's not necessarily true. Furthermore, and perhaps more dangerously, the simple act of measuring these things (or paying attention to them at all) will change how we think, work, lead, and communicate. It starts to change what we value and how we behave; we subconsciously want any metric we measure to go up. (Remember: what gets measured gets improved.)

For example, if we're measuring how many people go to our website, then it may lead us to send people to our website when they really don't need to go there. What if it's better to just send the info directly to them in a text or email? Without ever needing to click anything else or go to the website? That's a win. In this case, we don't care about web traffic. The metric we really care about is whether people get the information they need.

"Average time on page" is another common website metric. We assume it's better if that number is higher, meaning people are spending more time on our website. That's true if we are selling ads. But it's not true if the website visitor is just trying to find out what time they need to show up on Sunday. In that case, less time on the website is better. (It means they found the answer faster.)

It can be even worse with "likes," friends, followers, views, and pretty much every other metric built into today's media platforms. Yes, there are endless tips and tricks online on how to get more of each. But the question remains at the end: Does it matter? Have we accomplished the real goal we set out to accomplish? And do those metrics reflect genuine progress toward those goals? Sometimes they don't.

It's the same with the size of your email list, Sunday attendance, or dollars collected. I'm not saying we should totally ignore these metrics—they are often necessary to know and helpful in reaching our goals—but they are not the goal. If we don't want them leading us astray, we need to identify and focus most on the metrics that truly matter.

FIGURING OUT WHY

Find some kids to help you here, because they are always asking exactly the right question:

> Me: I want to get more traffic to the men's ministry page on the website.
> Kid: Why?

Me: Because I want to increase participation in our men's programs.

Kid: Why?

Me: Because men need to be united in their pursuit of wisdom, virtue, and holiness.

Kid: Why?

Me: So they can be better spiritual leaders.

If you want to get to the heart of the matter about something, just keep asking why. A few layers down you quickly get to what really matters. And it gives you a ton of insights about what you're really doing here and which metrics are worth measuring.

Now, admittedly, it may be more challenging to measure something like "How your men are improving as spiritual leaders." (It's worth a shot though!) But, regardless, what is absolutely essential is recognizing that the real goal is something very different than where we began—"more traffic to the men's ministry page." It's entirely possible to get more traffic to the men's ministry page and still do nothing meaningful to help men.

TAKING THE LONG VIEW

Ultimately, as we hope to address the bigger issues in the Church today and reverse the serious drift of people from our pews, choosing the right metrics is key. We must look at the broader trends over much larger timeframes and think multigenerationally.

How do we make disciples who make more disciples, who have children who become disciples that make disciples? We can't just win over the current generation; we must make it stick for generations, as the Church of antiquity has done for millennia. We know this requires stronger families, stable and unified churches, and enduring traditions (ways of living passed down from generations of ancestors) that contain wisdom beyond the limits of those of us who happen to be walking about. So take the long view when identifying the metrics that matter most at your church. Then be intentional about taking the steps to achieve those big goals. Stay focused. Do it on purpose.

REFLECT

- Are your current communications (everything posted in your bulletin, website, emails, announcements, etc.) achieving their goals right now? How are you regularly assessing their effectiveness?

- What are the metrics that matter most to you? How could you measure them better?

CHAPTER EIGHTEEN

Invitations That Work

Aristotle said, "A friend to all is a friend to no one." It's very similar with invitations: An invitation to all is like an invitation to no one. As churches, we want everyone to feel welcome and to know they're always invited (a beautiful and good thing). But that approach can actually hurt our cause if all our communications end up always inviting *everyone to everything*. At some point, the more people you invite to something, the fewer people respond.

THE INVITATION PARADOX

If you generically invite all one hundred people in the room to your birthday party, I won't feel very special and probably won't come. The invitation itself communicates that you don't necessarily want me in particular to come to your birthday party—just any ol' person will do. No thanks.

On the other hand, if you walk up to me personally and say, "Hey Matthew, would you like to come to my birthday party? I'd love to celebrate and catch up," I'm far more likely to go (especially if there is chocolate cake). In this case, you communicated that you wanted specifically me to be there.

The same dynamic happens when promoting church events. If we generically invite everyone with large group announcements, people won't feel personally wanted and welcome. If you want to get more people to show up to something, you might need to invite fewer people. That doesn't mean everything has to be a personal invitation (though that is usually the ideal and far more practical than we think). But any extra effort we make to invite specific groups of people for particular reasons communicates to those people that there is something special about them and that we think they would really enjoy whatever we're inviting them to. The more specifically an invitation is made to me, or my group, or people like me—the more special and relevant it feels—the more likely I am to respond in the affirmative.

That's one social dynamic to keep in mind when attempting to make invitations that work. But what other factors make an invitation successful?

SUCCESSFUL INVITATIONS DO THESE THINGS

Whether you are inviting somebody to attend an event, join the tribe, pay more attention, or take a step deeper into a relationship, there are four keys to doing it successfully. If your invitation isn't working, it's due to one of these four things.

1. TARGETING THE RIGHT PEOPLE

This seems a little too obvious, but people pitch great events to the wrong audience all the time and then wonder why nobody comes. The right target audience is foundational as to whether an invitation works.

So, first, take the time and make sure this invitation is right for this particular group. Second, remember the *invitation paradox.* The more people you invite at once, the less personal it is and the smaller the percentage that will respond. Do your best to direct the invitation to only the most appropriate sub-group within your community and make it as personal as possible. For example, don't invite a large group of mostly single people or kids to the marriage retreat. To the extent possible, make the invitation directly to people who are married.

2. EFFECTIVE DELIVERY

This step encompasses much of what we've covered throughout this book. Are you using the right channel for the occasion and format? Is it short and to the point, intriguing, relevant, creative, engaging, and even entertaining (which gets attention, keeps attention, and builds rapport)? Is it easy to respond and participate? Is there a clear next step? A common mistake is to just tell people what is happening but not what to do. Give them an obvious call to action (CTA). Make it clear what you want them to do.

For example, send a targeted email to the married couples of your community with a short, entertaining, convincing message that includes a two-minute testimonial video of a couple who attended last year. Include a simple button to "Learn more now" that takes them to your mobile-responsive website with a short signup form to pay and reserve a spot with ease.

3. THE CONVINCING "WHY"

This is the most important part. When making an invitation, don't start with what it is; start with *why* it's important. So don't say, "Come to our marriage retreat next month, it's all weekend long, costs $50, and will be held at the local retreat center." Instead, it's much smarter to say, "Is your spouse difficult to live with? Ever struggled to put your marriage ahead of your job, hobbies, or even your children? When was the last time you hit pause on life to focus on your marriage? Our annual marriage retreat is designed to help! Click here to learn more."

Leading with the details (the "what") before they even know whether they care about it or not is a sure recipe for glazed-over eyeballs. Instead, convince them why it matters first. Lead with something they are already looking for, struggling with, or thinking about. If you're convincing enough, then they'll be interested in all the other details and next steps that follow.

4. BARRIERS REMOVED

You may have these first three parts down perfectly—the right audience, the perfect delivery, and a very convincing *why*—but they still may not respond. There may still be barriers stopping them from coming. A great invitation anticipates barriers and proactively removes them if possible.

For instance, maybe they'd love to attend the marriage retreat but finding childcare is difficult. So you could offer childcare as part of the retreat. Maybe it's too expensive for some people, so offer discounts for those who need it. Maybe they'll be nervous about what to expect, so put them at ease about the experience. And if you're not sure what some of the barriers might be, it's very easy to find out: just ask them.

That goes for all of these. If your invitations aren't working, dig in and find out why. It will be due to one of these four keys to invitations that work. Analyze your invitation, break it down along these four parameters, and then address the areas that need help.

CHALLENGE

- What big event do you have coming up where you'd like to increase attendance?

- How would you use the four keys from this chapter to improve your invitation?

CHAPTER NINETEEN

The #1 Reason People Open Your Email (or Anything)

What is the real reason people open your email?

You know by now that it's not some kind of trick, like getting a software robot to insert the person's name into it. The effects of that trick have worn off and can make you look more like a spammy marketer than a leader people want to follow. Another tactic to definitely avoid is repeatedly *resending* the same email to everyone who hasn't opened it or responded yet. They may eventually open it all right, but it will probably be so they can mark it as spam and unsubscribe from it. (Remember: You can't make them listen!)

Let's apply the lessons from throughout this book. There are certainly some good things that provide marginal improvements to your open rates. Things like sending at the right time of day and week, finding the ideal sending frequency (according to what you've earned), making sure it's mobile-friendly, using better graphics, and keeping it short and packed with value—though don't overthink those things. One of the most significant things you can do to increase email open rates is spend time creating a great subject line (the headline). That is often worth putting a little extra effort into. (Go to whytheyfollow.com/subjectlines to listen to our podcast episode on writing great subject lines for churches.) But honestly, the impact of all these ideas is still insignificant compared to the #1 reason people open your email.

It turns out the #1 reason people open your email is the same reason they'll open just about anything (a piece of mail, invitations, a present, the door, etc.): *relationship*. (Because they know your voice, remember?)

The "from name" is the most important factor in whether somebody opens your email. And I don't mean coming up with a clever "from name" that displays in their inbox. I mean who are *you* (the sender) to *them* (the reader)? What's your relationship? Are you the person leading them somewhere meaningful? And what has been the quality of your relationship via this particular channel up to this point?

Think about your own inbox. You quickly scan down and jump to the emails from people or organizations whose relationships you value most. (Sure, a great subject line will catch your attention sometimes too, but not before the from name and not consistently.)

A LITTLE BETTER OR A LOT BETTER?

If you'd like to increase your average engagement or open rates a little bit—for example, from 20% to 26%—sure, try using advanced metrics and split testing software and all those other tactics I mentioned. But if, instead, you want to take your open rate from 20% to 60%+ consistently every time (and not fuss with all those other tactics), then build a deep, meaningful relationship with your people. Put something big at stake. Convince them to buy into the mission you're on and the story you're in and to own their place in the tribe. Go somewhere big and bold and meaningful together. Then they'll not only open your next email but look forward to it. They'll anticipate it. They'll be sad when they check their inbox and it's not there yet because they can't wait to see what's going to happen next.

IT'S ALREADY BAKED IN ·

A key lesson here is that the biggest factors—which will impact the open rate of the email you send today—have already all been determined prior to today. They've already happened. It's every little thing you've done up to this point to build a good relationship with this person. There is little you're going to do today to change the performance of today's email. Instead, take the long view and know that today is a chance to build a slightly better relationship, increase trust, further enroll them in the journey, and ultimately earn the permission to speak to them again tomorrow or the next day. Do that consistently and open rates will go up.

TIPS FOR GETTING PEOPLE TO READ YOUR STUFF

Note: I'm talking a lot about email in this chapter, but virtually all of this applies to any communication channel you use—announcements, email, bulletin, text messaging, social media, website, etc.

1. Does the person really know you? Have you spent time building a personal relationship with each person in your group? The more you build genuine personal relationships, the more likely people are to open your communications.

2. Is it always worth their time? What has your email (or whatever channel) relationship been like up until now? Are your messages short and to the point? Are they always packed with only the most important content? Are they always relevant to this person? Have you shown them that your messages are always worth their time?

3. Segment your audience when you communicate. Avoid saying everything to everyone, and only send the right information to the right groups of people. (This is one

of the key ways to dramatically increase the chance that people will regularly find your messages relevant.)

4. Be a person. People don't have relationships with buildings or organizations; they have relationships with other people. Write as a person, from a person. You can be professional and serious but still have fun and let your personality shine. Let your joy come through no matter what channel you're using.

5. Are your communications all about you? Too many organizations use their communication channels to only promote themselves (their events, their campaigns, their thoughts, etc.). Then they wonder why people stop listening or reading. As inspiring and important as your work is, people don't sign up for your information or visit your website to only hear about you. They want to do something meaningful. They want to be helped. They want to hear about others. They want to be asked about themselves and listened to. They want to have fun. They want to be inspired. They want to be engaged. They want to contribute. They want to receive things that are practical and useful for their lives. They want to make a real and personal connection with you. Only about one-tenth of your communications should be you telling them

what you want them to know. The rest should be all this other stuff.

6. Put something big at stake. I have to reiterate this because it is the biggest factor by far. Are you leading them on a mission to achieve a big thing that they care about? If so, they will be anticipating your next communication, ready to jump down to it and read it as soon as it hits their inbox. Make clear that everything you are doing and communicating, even the little, seemingly trivial things, is connected to achieving something meaningful that they care about. Otherwise, why does it matter how many people open our emails in the first place?

ASSESS

- What is your current average email open rate? (Your email tool should be automatically measuring this for you.)

- What could you try this year that could improve that open rate by 10% (for example, go from 30% to 40%)?

CHAPTER TWENTY

Asking for Money

What if you could raise $420,000 in three weeks . . . with three simple emails? And do it at a small church the size of 180 (mostly middle-class) families? That's precisely what we did at my parish, Presentation of the Lord Catholic Church. We needed to raise $1,000,000 to expand the chapel. Here's how we hit that goal and the keys to our success.

As you turn into the still signless entrance to our property and pull down the potholed driveway, you pass a little house and come to an old, nondescript metal box of a building (the previous property owner's workshop). The new little cross on top lets you know you're in the right place. It's not much yet, but there is a big, inspiring vision. And our pastor, Fr. Justin Fletcher, has done a good job the past couple years of communicating that vision. One of the first things he did was develop a master plan. The plan includes a beautiful gothic-style church, a large cemetery, contemplative nuns, a parish hall to host community events, and plenty of room for children to run free.

THE IMPORTANCE OF THE BIG VISION

A master plan helps people visualize something concrete, but it represents far more than just exciting new buildings. There is a real urgency in our community that we need this. God wants more thriving, growing churches. Our families need this. Our children need this. And by creating such an extraordinary place, we can better nourish families, more successfully pass on the faith to the next generation, and help more people get to heaven. Big things are at stake. Real things. It matters.

Fr. Fletcher has repeatedly communicated, "We want to do something where—centuries from now—people will look at it and say, 'Wow, these people sure loved God!'" The vision includes evangelizing people hundreds of years from now. And we're building a community that is fruitful in every sense of the word, producing more children than adults (which translates to tremendous hope) and giving people the opportunity to be part of something bigger than ourselves—directly carrying on the mission of Jesus' Apostles from two thousand years ago. All of that is incredibly meaningful to people. The chance to be part of something that significant doesn't come along often. So people jump at the opportunity to help.

BIG GIFTS AND PERSONAL RELATIONSHIPS

Before we ever even announced the campaign to everyone to raise $1,000,000, our pastor was able to first quietly raise $580,000 of it from six or seven large donors, all but one of whom were already parishioners. That makes the $420,000 chunk raised later even more impressive because it didn't include the largest donors in the parish. Keep in mind, this was a parish of families who had already dug deep into their pockets. A few years before, they had raised money to buy twenty-three acres of land, and regular offertory contributions were already above average compared to other churches.

So how did Fr. Fletcher raise the $580,000 (58% of the goal) before even announcing the campaign? First, he regularly and openly communicated the genuine needs of the parish. The first $100,000 check came from somebody who already knew we needed to expand the chapel and wanted to get the ball rolling. Second, multiple others came from people who had mentioned to him in the past, "When you need money to do the next thing, let me know." They were inspired by the vision and wanted to support it. Third, because he had spent years getting to know his flock, he had a good idea of the people who would be able to make a large donation and so could directly ask them for what we needed. But the key foundation to raising the early money from large donors (alongside God's providence of course) was Fr. Fletcher's tireless effort of building personal relationships, repeatedly communicating needs, and truly getting to know his flock.

All of this made actually launching the campaign far easier. We started off 58% finished on day one, already well on our way to a clearly achievable goal. It also communicated that large donors were totally on board with the plan, which inspired more confidence still. All of that, combined with repeated communication of the vision and what was at stake, earned a wide consensus of buy-in from the community for the project.

CONNECTING THE DOTS

Some people asked, "Why are we putting $1,000,000 into expanding this little chapel when we have plans to build a bigger, more beautiful church building as part of the master plan?" Before people would buy into this campaign, they needed to see how this particular project was connected to the big vision. It was critical to explain that we were out of space right now on Sunday, and that if we wanted to eventually afford the master plan, we needed to create room for more people to join our community first.

Many projects are like that; they may seem pointless or trivial to others until you connect the dots for them. Then they see how those baby steps in the middle are actually the pathway to the place they want to go.

A SENSE OF OWNERSHIP

We're blessed with a community that has a real sense of ownership and affection for our church. Fr. Fletcher described a general attitude among the parishioners of "This is my place, and I want to see it thrive." If people settle for a mere transactional relationship with their church—I go here to give a little something, get a little something, then leave—then they're generally happy with the status quo. But if it's yours and you love it and it becomes a part of your identity, an opportunity to show gratitude, and a deep expression of God's fruitfulness in your life, then you are willing to make big sacrifices to make it as good as you possibly can. Certainly our smaller size, commitment to transparency, and pioneering spirit has contributed to a natural sense of ownership. But I think it mostly comes from the mesh network of personal relationships that have been forged and nourished at our parish. Many of our closest friend groups, our family members, and our children's social groups are all there for coffee and donuts on Sunday, as well as many other communal events, feasts, and volunteer opportunities all rooted in and around the liturgy.

It's always a good practice to ask for people's time before asking for their money. Get them involved. Build personal relationships with them first. Allow them to develop a sense of ownership and an affection for your community. The money flows more naturally after that.

MAKING THE PROCESS EASY

This was the final piece to the puzzle that made our ask so successful: We made it extremely easy for people to pledge. Here's the pledge card we used:

CHAPEL EXPANSION PROJECT

ALREADY GIVEN: $580,000 | STILL NEEDED: $420,000 | COST $1,000,000

WE NEED YOUR HELP

INCLUDES
- Narthex (w/ bathrooms)
- Additional seating
- New property access road
- City water connect for future campus
- Landscaping

HOW TO MAKE A PLEDGE

Simply click the link sent out in our weekly parish email. That's it.

You can also pledge at:
presentation.church/pledge

HELP US EXPAND OUR CHAPEL

Our parish goal is to provide a stable, enduring, and beautiful place where heaven and earth touch and man is reconciled to God. This expansion not only allows for more growth and needed amenities, it takes the next step in securing our wonderful home for generations to come as a place of sanctuary and splendor. By meeting our goal we can complete the project debt-free, and position ourselves well for the next phase of transforming earth into heaven.

Any size gift helps, but to reach our goal we'll need something like:

40 families to give $1,000	(or $50/month for 20 months)
40 families to give $5,000	(or $250/month for 20 months)
15 families to give $10,000	(or $500/month for 20 months)
5 families to give $20,000	(or $1000/month for 20 months)

The pledge cards were just so we could put something physical in their hands on Sunday. We didn't collect pledges that way. We used the pledging feature built right into Flocknote, which allows people to click a button in an email and then make a pledge in literally a few clicks, without having to create accounts, log in anywhere, or re-enter all their information. It is a game changer. It even automatically sends follows-ups and reminders for pledges that fall behind on payments.

Once we launched the campaign, we announced it each Sunday and handed out the pledge cards. We sent one email per week with the link to click to quickly make a pledge. After three weeks, we had crossed the $1,000,000 finish line (and soon after hit $1.2 million). Over 50% of families pledged, almost 100% of which were already regular donors.

ZERO TRICKS

So if you want to know how we could send three emails over three weeks and hit such a huge goal with such a small community, it's because we did all of that first. We didn't use any gimmicks or tricks. We used zero social media. We didn't need any wealth-screening tools or harvested demographic data about our community. We didn't need to auto-insert people's names into the emails we sent to make them appear more personal.

People give their money to things for the same reasons they open your communications or give their time and energy to anything: because they are enrolled in the cause, led by somebody who has earned their trust. Because they care about what's at stake. Because they are true followers, excited to go where you are leading them. Raising money from people like that is pretty straightforward (and even fun!). On the other hand, trying to raise money from folks who haven't yet enrolled in the cause (the situation many development offices find themselves in) is often a long, hard, frustrating slog. The point? Get people truly following first.

BEFORE YOU ASK FOR MONEY

Most of what determines your success in asking for money happens long before you ask. It's like sowing any seed—most of the work is in first cultivating the soil. The bulk of how to do that has been covered elsewhere in this book, but here are a few specific reminders and tips for asking for money:

1. **Vision and leadership are paramount:** I won't belabor the point too much, since I've mentioned it throughout the book and already in this chapter. But I can't create this list of tips and not have it listed first. If you've ever had to listen to somebody ask for money from the pulpit, head down, reading a prepared statement too fast, with no emotion, no pauses, no eye contact, wishing the awkward moment was over as soon as possible, it's because they knew the room was filled with people who were not yet enrolled in the cause. The more people have bought into the vision and your plan, the more they will literally buy into it with their hard-earned dollars.

2. **Invest in personal relationships:** There is no shortcut for this. There are so many untapped resources (time, talent, treasure) sitting in the pews, but the best way to connect the dots back to the needs is to get out there and get to know people.

3. Communicate your value: The months and years leading up to the "ask" should be spent continually communicating the value that your ministry provides to your community. Most of your communications in general should be doing this in one way or another. Repeatedly give generously to them first. Then when it's time to ask for something, it comes from within the context of a generous and giving relationship. If the only time I hear from you outside of normal channels is to ask me for money, don't expect much.

4. The right-sized goal: This is certainly an art, but setting the right-sized goal is very important. You want something attainable for the community but still challenging. How big of a step can we take together right now? How motivated is everyone? How many big donors do we have? How many total families? How's the economy? And how deeply have they already dug into their pockets? How much do we need now, and how much can be collected over future installments? Most of that comes from genuinely knowing your flock. Then the answers to these questions become more intuitive.

5. Regularly communicate your needs: Be transparent about what your ongoing needs are and don't be shy about sharing them. Maybe somebody in the pew already has the solution or is particularly motivated to donate the money for it themselves (before you even have to ask!).

6. Good past performance: How have you handled their money in the past? Have you proven to be a good steward of it? Did you do what you said you would do? And did you express gratitude?

7. Define your campaign creatively: If some of your income is fungible (like general offertory, etc., which can be spent at your discretion), use those funds for all your boring stuff (paying debt, fixing roof gutters, replacing the plumbing, new office equipment for staff, etc.). Save the things that most directly impact people (generally more fun stuff) for your fundraising campaigns. These are the things people will be most motivated and excited to give money toward—like a new church building, donuts, more comfortable pews, or a playground for the kids.

8. Bundling is smart: If you do need to raise money for something boring (like a new plumbing or irrigation system), consider bundling the fundraising goal together with something more visible and fun, like a baptismal font or a fountain for the courtyard. Then people will be more excited to give money since it includes something they can look forward to seeing and enjoying.

When you ask:

1. Be clear about the problem (and what's at stake): Be clear and honest about what problem you are trying to solve. Don't just say, "We need more parking." Say, "We have many people who want to be a part of what we're doing but can't because there's no room for them to park, so they are leaving and not coming back." Be concrete. It's incredible what people are capable of when they really know what's at stake (and it matters to them). So don't just say we're raising money for the seminary to pay its bills. Say, "If we don't get $150,000 by next month, three seminarians will have to be sent home." Even better, share the personal stories of those seminarians. If we leave it ambiguous, people assume it's probably not a big deal, and if they don't give, some other rich person waiting in the wings will probably cover it.

2. Emphasize the why: Don't forget you still have to remind people why solving this problem even matters. Don't assume they know, even if it's obvious to you. Why does it matter if we have fewer seminarians? Why do we care if people can't find a place to park and just go home instead? Get to the heart of the matter and connect it to your bigger vision and mission.

3. Communicate the plan: Research the problem you're trying to solve, understand your options, and have a detailed plan of how the money will be spent. Good planning informs many important decisions along the way, but it also gives people confidence in your leadership (that they want to go where you're going and believe you can get them there). Big donors especially want to know you have a responsible plan for their money before writing that big check.

4. Ask for what you need: Don't get shy when it's time to ask for money. If you don't tell people how much you need from them, it's hard for them to know how deep they need to dig. You can see an easy way to do this for a mixed group in the pledge card example above. A good leader simply must be able to explain that "we need $X if we want to achieve Y. And that means we need each family to give something like $Z." If you're feeling nervous about asking, it's likely because you sense you haven't yet earned the right to ask (i.e., enrolled them in the cause).

5. It's not about you: People are not very motivated to make you the hero (the one who flies in to save the day, solving this problem). They want to be the hero themselves. (We all do!) So when you communicate, make it clear that we need them to step up, be the hero, and make this happen. You are just there to help them do it.

6. Get the CTA (Call to Action) right: Be clear about what you want them to do, and make participating easy.

Keep pledge cards (or online forms) short. Don't ask for information that isn't truly necessary. The more hoops somebody has to jump through to give money, the less they'll participate. Make the process quick, with clear instructions and an easy way to pay. Your online giving software must be simple and user-friendly. All of this applies whether you are announcing it in person, putting it in an email, or communicating it any other way.

7. Have fun: That's right, it should be fun. If it's not, you likely skipped some of the steps above. Though it often requires great sacrifice, giving money is rewarding and feels good . . . that is, if it's connected to doing something big and meaningful. You must help your people look past the hard, awkward, not-so-fun part of getting asked for and giving money, and on toward what it's all for! You are not burdening them; you are giving them a chance at a more meaningful life—a way to give their hearts to God (Matt. 6:21).

8. Leverage the right communication channels: In-person announcements can be, by far, the most human and compelling. So make them really good! But often the transition from your pitch to them paying (making a gift) is more difficult when in-person. So you should also send them an electronic follow-up (email or text message) with a link to give, where they can pay in a few clicks.

9. Say different things to different people: There is already a whole chapter on this, but this is especially important when asking for money. Make sure your software can help with this when it comes to fundraising. With Flocknote, you can sort folks by things like which funds they've given to, how much they've already given, and how recently they've given, and then combine that with other data, like how involved they are, the last time they opened an email, etc. Then you can really cater your message to be most effective for the various segments of your flock.

10. Say thank you often: It's free to say and makes a huge difference. Create a culture of generosity and gratitude that flows both ways.

REFLECT

- When was the last time you showed your flock what their generosity has accomplished in the world?

- How do you regularly and clearly communicate your church's needs to your community?

- How easy is it for somebody to give money to your church? (Can they do it online and from their phone? Do they have to reenter payment information each time? Do they have to remember a password to log in? Etc.)

CHAPTER TWENTY-ONE

Don't Say It; Do It

The early Christians risked extremely high chances of death and imprisonment to live their faith. A young boy, St. Tarcisius, was martyred in the third century while bravely attempting to sneak the Eucharist in to imprisoned Christians who desired the Lord more than anything else. Throughout all of history (and even still today), Christians have lived where the faith is illegal, risking their lives to receive the sacraments and read Scripture and regularly walking many treacherous miles just to see a priest.

What does this willingness to risk something for God communicate more powerfully than anything else? What message do such actions send? A timelessly inspiring one that reverberates down to us still to this day, thousands of years later. Whether by the red martyrdom of shedding our own blood or the white martyrdom of slowly dying to self in daily service to those around us, we are all called to communicate that same message in that same radical way.

WORDS AS CRUTCHES

It sounds funny, but words can easily become crutches when communicating. It's easier to say something than do something, and it's tempting to take that shortcut. But it's always more effective to show rather than tell. And the truth is, our work shouldn't really need a lot of explaining.

If you are in the presence of a great lion, nobody needs to explain that he's powerful and dangerous. Observe his claws. Watch him move. Hear him roar. You'll know he's dangerous because every hair on your body is screaming it. Our communicating should be more like that. More roaring, less explaining.

TRY THIS

Stop explaining how easy and fun something is. Just make it easy and fun. Don't insist on the goodness of your work; just do good. Don't describe its beauty; show it. Don't tell them it's meaningful; just make their life more meaningful.

Don't talk about the new website; do something truly useful with it. Don't ask people to sign up for a new tool (it's not about the tool); ask them to join you in doing something meaningful (use the tool to help). Don't say I have a few announcements; just announce them. Don't say I have a question; just ask. Don't talk about how you're doing pastoral planning; just execute the plan.

Don't say it; do it. You might be surprised at how effective you become at communicating. They say people would rather see a sermon than hear one. Well, here's a fun exercise to try. Take something that you wish your flock understood or valued more and ask, "How could we communicate the importance of this particular thing *without using words*?" You can only use actions. What would you do? Get creative.

THE LOUDEST MESSAGE YOU COMMUNICATE

Mother Teresa (now a canonized saint) spoke beautiful, simple, and powerful words. But it was her extreme sacrifice and the radical way in which she ordered her life that roared most loudly and shook people to their core—without having to say a word. All the saints are like that. If you want to know the loudest message you are communicating to the people around you, it has less to do with the words you say and much more to do with the answer to these two questions: (1) What do you make the biggest sacrifices for? (2) What is your entire life ordered around?

If we make bigger sacrifices for our career than for our family, then we communicate that career is more important than family (no matter what words we say to the contrary). If we can stay up late for the big game but can't get up for church, then we communicate that sports are more important than church. If we manage to fit in hours of TV each day but no time for prayer, then we communicate that TV is more important than God. If we spend more time talking about college prep with our kids than about their faith, then . . . well, you get the point.

What we say out loud is a very small part of what we ultimately end up communicating. The actions we take, the sacrifices we make, the entire way that we order and structure our lives—these become the bulk of the message we ultimately end up communicating.

COMMUNICATING WHAT YOU LOVE

I have six kids, which means I've spent a lot of time repeating things that just repeatedly get ignored. As my children have gotten older, I've learned that while they don't always hear what I say very well, they do hear loudly what I love.

We worry a lot about saying the right things and giving them the right advice. But the whole time the message being shouted at them is in what I love. Not what I tell them I love, but what my actions show them that I love. What do I make the biggest sacrifices for? And what do I order my life around?

What gets communicated is what we love. Children see that. They feel it. They sense it. That's the message they receive. We can tell them how to love their neighbor, but they will learn what that means by watching how we love ours. We can tell them too much screen time is bad for you, but if every time they look up they see us looking at a screen, guess what they will grow up and do? We can tell them that our faith is the most important thing in our lives, but if they don't see that we've completely reordered our entire lives around God and what is most likely to get us to heaven, then they won't believe our words.

We communicate what we love. It's the same when leading your flock.

WHATEVER YOU CAN DO

The COVID-19 pandemic and the subsequent various levels of lockdowns it caused presented a lot of challenges for churches—but also opportunities. Tina Gregory, Communications Director at St. Michael Catholic Church, said that when they didn't even want them getting out of their cars, and they were fully locked down, their pastor said, "Well, then we'll do a parking lot Benediction [blessing with the Eucharist] and Eucharistic procession." In other words, what can we do? We'll do that. That very willingness to do whatever they could, despite the inconvenience and sacrifice, communicated loudly that *what we do here is essential*. Your spiritual life is important. God is important. Being together (to whatever extent possible) is important.

"There wasn't a parking space left," continued Tina. "People were double parked . . . and even encouraging people to park in front of them. There were bells. There was incense. And people were in tears. People were opening their car doors and kneeling on the pavement; it was glorious!" That later turned into drive-thru Confessions and Communion and doing whatever prudence allowed. But the point is that they were willing to be flexible, creative, and jump through as many hoops as it took to do whatever was possible. That communicates a powerful message.

A SENSE OF PURPOSE

John F. Kennedy was known for his sense of purpose. When he entered the room, people knew they had just encountered a man on a mission. Most great leaders have this.

How they speak, the look in their eye, their posture, their energy, their whole demeanor—it all conveys a great sense of purpose. It all communicates that this person is serious about doing something meaningful. You feel like at any moment something big could happen, and you don't want to miss it. You want to join their tribe so you can be a part of it. They are passionate and capable. You want to go where they are going, and you believe they can take you there.

This sense of purpose doesn't come from having a particularly strong commitment to an external goal. It comes, rather, from the aligning of one's identity with a particular task or mission. In other words, it's what God put you on this Earth to do. If we are to be great leaders, we must achieve a similar alignment and clarity of purpose, through much prayer and discernment. Once we have an authentic sense of our own purpose, communicating it becomes almost automatic, because people can sense it in our very being, who we are, and how we naturally behave.

SHOW, DON'T TELL

As a last resort, when you can't communicate it by doing it, at least try to say it in a way that shows. Use videos, sounds, pictures, and stories.

It's a huge missed opportunity when, for example, at the end of the year, a person gets a spreadsheet from their church that says, "Here's what we did with your money this year." The spreadsheets are important, but it's not what motivates people. Instead, what if I got a two-minute testimonial video of Bob, whose family was able to have a proper Thanksgiving dinner this year due to the generosity of our church? Or I got pictures of the smiling faces of the children enjoying the playground our money helped build? Or I heard the story of somebody whose life was recently changed after attending our church?

Cristina Folan, Director of Communications at Notre Dame Mt. Carmel, has adopted this approach and hasn't looked back. She said their communications have moved away from just announcing events and have instead focused on "What's happening as a result of those events? What is going on? How are people doing?" and telling those stories. She started interviewing people, recording conversations, and sharing them through Flocknote, simply asking people to describe their experiences and how they've been transformed by them. She also takes lots of pictures to share along with these stories. Doing this every week has been a "wonderful change in culture" and a much better way to communicate with and engage the flock.

Emily Urban from St. Christopher's was asked to get up and speak on Sunday about raising money to repair their aging church building. She wasn't sure how to go about doing it, so she just had fun with it and told her own story of aging. She said, "My husband here has had to replace two knees and one hip. I've had to replace a few teeth, and recently, even my prosthetic eye. But with some maintenance, I think we clean up pretty good! But I need to do this for my parish too. I'm here to tell you that my husband and I are going to increase what we give. We've been blessed. We need upkeep, and so does God's house. I invite you to do as we're doing." And guess what? Giving went up enough to cover the needed repairs.

Stories are incredibly powerful and perhaps the most natural way humans communicate. Stories draw people in and are far more engaging. Stories show. And when those stories come from within their own community, it reminds them that they are already in the middle of a meaningful story right now that is unfolding before them. And, Cristina added, even if somebody isn't directly involved in these stories yet, those people still begin to claim these stories as part of their own: "There's a sense that 'I belong to this.'" And it reminds us all that people "don't come to church for a transaction. They come to church to go on a journey, and for an experience."

Don't just tell them with words. Show them what they're a part of. Show them how much you care by what you're willing to sacrifice for it. Show them how important it is by completely reordering your life around it. Show them what their money and sacrifices are accomplishing. Show them evidence that you're achieving your mission in a meaningful way. Show them the difference they are making. Show them the tangible impact their contribution has made. Tell them the story of the people they've helped. Remind them what was (and still remains) at stake. Do that and people will beg you for ways to go out and help do even more of it.

ASSESS

- Aliens just landed at your church. If they watch what you do on Sunday morning (not knowing the language), what would they conclude is most important to you? What is being communicated by your actions?

- Read one of your recent communications. How could you do more showing rather than telling?

CHAPTER TWENTY-TWO

Hangups, Hurdles, and Help

As we near the end of the book, I hope by now you've got a good list of things going that you'd like to try or implement for your church or ministry. But you may also be having some of the following thoughts or feelings:

- Where do I start?
- I don't have time to try these things.
- My boss won't let me do any of this.
- I'm overwhelmed!

Or you may be feeling tempted to take on too much, try to change things too quickly, set unrealistic expectations, or get distracted by less important (but more fun) ideas. Well, here are some things to keep in mind that will help.

I DON'T HAVE TIME

Lack of prayer leads to lack of time.
—Peter Kreeft

Many people think they don't pray enough because they don't have enough time. But it's actually the other way around. They don't have enough time because they don't pray enough.

One of the most convenient excuses for taking shortcuts or not doing something is "I don't have time." But lack of time is never a problem when we are doing God's will.

If we are praying enough, we begin to clearly see God's plan for us today. And it just so happens that, of course, God has provided plenty of time for his plan. It's all the other stuff we try to cram in instead that we don't have time for. You don't have time for both your plan and God's. You must choose which one you want more.

And yet, even when choosing God's plan, we must be faithful enough to do it on his time. God's plan is, indeed, to accomplish big things and prosper us. But our job is not to demand it now; rather it is simply to not give up before it happens. A patient person allows God the space (in time as it were) to work according to God's time rather than our own. Fr. Pierre Teilhard de Chardin says that we must "trust in the slow work of God," and not try to be today "what time (that is to say, grace and circumstances acting on your own good will) will make of you tomorrow."

Our lives are too busy, but they don't have to be. People often confuse busy with productive. And they confuse productive with important. Much of our busyness is not productive. And much of our productivity is not important.

And even then, there are endless important, good things we can spend our time on today. But we don't have time to do them all. So what do we do? How do we know which important thing to do today and which to leave off doing for another time? In the end, it's not time that we lack at all; it's clarity. And clarity comes from prayer. Find that clarity and you'll also find that you have everything you need—including plenty of time.

MY BOSS WON'T LET ME

Your boss or pastor may not see the value in trying something new. The key to winning them (or anyone else) over is to start with something they care about. Sometimes we want to try something new because we like new things or because other people are doing it. It's a leader's job to make sure we are being intentional about the changes we make.

So if your boss won't let you do something, first consider that maybe they are right. Have we clearly identified the value in trying this new thing? Is it really worthwhile? If it's not, then of course we shouldn't waste our time. If it is, however, the next question is: "Have we successfully communicated that value to my boss in a way that is meaningful *to them*?"

The key to doing that is to start with something they care about and then show them how the change or new tool will help achieve that. It's pretty simple. Ask them what they are passionate about, find out what their goals are for this year, and then show them how your new approach or technology is going to help them reach those goals. If it actually helps them (and you can prove it), there's a good chance they'll be on board.

If you say, "Pastor, we really need to be able to text message our folks any time we want. It's what everyone is doing these days," then I wouldn't blame them for hesitating. You haven't yet presented a convincing "why" or communicated the value.

If, on the other hand, you say, "Pastor, if we could text message our members the night before your event to remind them about it, we would double our attendance the next day," now you'll have their interest. Then be sure to also include a plan to test it out and report back the actual results to them in the future. Do that, and I bet you'll get a much more positive response.

Basically, you're just inviting them to something—you're inviting them to try something new. So look back at chapter 18 on invitations that work and apply it to this invitation. You'll have much more success.

DOING THE WORK

*Opportunity is missed by most people because it is
dressed in overalls and looks like work.*

—Thomas Edison

We tend to romanticize leadership. We see successful leaders as charismatic, famous, brilliant, charming, naturally effective, fearless, courageous people who change the world doing big, important things. Most leaders aren't really like that. And they certainly don't start off like that.

Instead, becoming a great leader has more to do with just getting up every day and doing things we don't feel like doing. If we do that every day for a long time, progress is made. We may even become more charismatic, effective, and courageous in the process. Most days, that's what leading the flock toward our big vision looks like.

But we're human, and we don't feel like doing hard things *today* (tomorrow sounds much better). I'm as guilty of this as anyone. When it comes time to do the hard work, we check our email one more time. We check Instagram again. We check a few more small to-dos off the list. We do another survey, ask another committee, watch another video, or buy another book to teach us something else we need to know first. We look for anything that can delay the effort or give us hope of getting out of it. That's when the temptation for taking shortcuts is at its peak too.

Steven Pressfield calls this derailing force in the universe "the Resistance." Christians know it is actually three different things: "the world, the flesh, and the devil," all working against us in different ways. But whatever you call it, this Resistance actually gets stronger and stronger the closer and closer you get to doing something great. That's why they say *life gets tougher toward the summit.* So when you are in the business of doing big things, you must learn to overcome the Resistance, because it is going to come at you hard—especially when you're right near the finish line or on the verge of a big breakthrough.

> *Procrastination is the most common manifestation*
> *of Resistance because it's the easiest to rationalize.*
> *We don't tell ourselves, "I'm never going to write my*
> *symphony." Instead we say, "I am going to write my*
> *symphony; I'm just going to start tomorrow."*
> —Steven Pressfield

IF YOU WANT TO DO IT

If you want to do it, then you have to do it.
—My dad

It took me many years to realize that my dad wasn't only being funny when he'd say that. He's an athlete and extremely hard worker—a doer. And he knows the biggest secret to getting stuff done: *just do it*. He must have been onto something, since years later Nike made it one of the most popular slogans in the world.

Fitness is the example par excellence to which most of us can relate. We spend thousands of dollars on special exercise equipment, gym memberships, workout clothes, fitness trainers, innovative diets, and creative regimens. Do you know which one is the best? The one you'll actually do. The truth is, you don't really need any of that to get in shape and be healthy. Put your shoes on, open the door, and start running. Don't eat too much, and eat mostly real food. Whatever the workout, whatever the diet, the key is you just have to do it. And then keep doing it, even if it starts to feel boring. Yes, it's hard. But that's the secret. That's it. It's the same with accomplishing most big things in life. There are those who dream about what could be, and there are those that go out and get to work.

ON OVERNIGHT SUCCESS

Most "overnight success stories"—once you really dig into them—actually took about ten years. It's rare that big things are accomplished quickly. They take patience, hard work, and slogging away at it day after day, little by little.

I know that's been our experience here at Flocknote. We've grown tremendously fast, but it took about ten years of slow, hard work, during which a big competitor could have pushed us out at any moment. Now, what feels like suddenly, it's very different, and we work with ten thousand churches. But it took about ten years of plugging away at it before we really felt like we had succeeded.

Your destiny as a leader of your church is not hanging on finding the right advice today on a YouTube channel. It will be decided by what you intentionally set out to do over the next ten years to master your craft and lead your flock toward your big vision. What will it be? Where do you want to be in ten years? Now start today. Find one small thing that moves you closer. Tomorrow, do it again. And be willing to be patient, put in the work, and enjoy the journey. Archbishop Fulton Sheen wasn't called "the great communicator" by Billy Graham because he winged it. He reportedly spent an average of thirty hours preparing for one hour of TV. And later in life, when asked how long it took him to prepare for a particular sermon, he famously responded, "Forty years."

KEEP IT SIMPLE

Simplicity is the ultimate sophistication.
—Leonardo da Vinci

Do you know what feels just as good as checking something off your to-do list? Deleting it off your list entirely. Want a real shortcut that actually works? Do less.

You don't need to do as much as you think. What if you did less but did it better? What if you only focused on the most important things and hit pause on the rest? What if we stopped viewing our lives in terms of all the things we aren't getting done (which are infinite) and instead focused on doing one big thing to heroic proportion?

They say we tend to overestimate what we can do in one year and underestimate what we can do in ten years. I think that's because we tend to be too ambitious and impatient. We like the idea of achieving it all now. (Heck, I don't even know if I want six-pack abs in ten years!)

So what do we do? We pile on too much and then make little real progress on any one particular thing. Over time, as I've learned to put less on my to-do list, I've actually accomplished more.

THE 25/5 RULE

The 25/5 rule is amazing at helping you do less. Here's how it works:

1. Make a list of the top twenty-five things you want to accomplish in life (or at work).
2. Circle the top five most important.
3. Cross everything else off the list (and put them on your AVOID-AT-ALL-COSTS list).

The point is that if you try to do all twenty-five, you may not accomplish any of them. But if you pick just five, you have a real shot of doing them (then you can pick five more after that of course). But the key principle is understanding that we have to say "no" to way more things than we think (even perhaps many of the things you picked up from this book). We can't do it all. But if we are content to focus on just a few, we just might succeed.

THE 80/20 RULE

The 80/20 rule (aka the Pareto Principle) is another rule every leader should understand. It's a helpful way of characterizing the disproportionality between causes and effects in life. It states that 80% of outcomes typically come from 20% of causes. And we can see it on display everywhere:

- 20% of your volunteers do 80% of the work.
- 20% of the flock gives 80% of the money. (It's actually worse than that.)
- 20% of your members give you 80% of the complaints.
- 20% of your kids give you 80% of the heartache.

You get the idea. But this is also true for your work. 80% of the impact your work is going to have will come from 20% of your actions. Do those first. Or try this: 80% of your stress right now is coming from 20% of your to-dos. Start there. What if you could do 20% of your tasks and reduce your stress by 80%? What if you could do 20% of your work and achieve 80% of the results? You can.

Look at your list of to-dos and circle the 20% that are going to deliver a disproportionately large amount of value. (They are often the ones you feel least like doing.) But look into the future at the end of your day/week/year and ask yourself, "Which of these tasks will I be most happy to have completed?" Do those and forget the rest for now.

It's a funny thing. If we shoot for 100%, we often fall dreadfully short. But if we are okay with just hitting 80% first, we can get there with 20% of the work and still typically end up better off.

Don't overcomplicate your life. Focus. Make it count. Do less, and achieve more.

BIG VISION, INCREMENTAL STEPS

Finally, with all of these, be patient and don't move too fast. Cultivating soil takes time. Don't try to move faster than the speed of grace. And even when we find a way in with people, it's essential that we propose, not impose, and inspire, not require. Leave room for your people to progress naturally and claim each step as their own. Think incrementally, like compound interest. Small gains compounding over time have the biggest impact in the end.

You must take your big vision and then break it down into baby steps to get there. Otherwise it's easy to get overwhelmed and just do nothing. Break it down into doable chunks. Then just do the first thing, updating the plan as you go (and as God reveals it to you).

Incremental steps are also important for meeting each of your people where they're at. This is the idea of "next steps." Start with something a person cares about right now and help them take a step toward something bigger. That journey is unique for each individual, which is why your leadership must be personal. If you try to shortcut that process and force them all along at the same pace as one big group, you'll probably fail.

Working incrementally is powerful and an amazing way to offload a ton of stress. Don't bear the stress of tomorrow's work today. You don't have to do it all at once. Just do a little bit. Then build on that. If we're persistent, the compounding effect is tremendous.

Consider that about 7% of a church's members do almost all of the volunteering and financial giving. Now, of course, thinking about how to engage the other 93% all at once is overwhelming. What if this year—instead of 93%—you just focused on getting 1% more? For a church with one thousand families, 1% is just ten families! What if your priority this year was to get ten more families fully engaged? Sounds very doable, right? And you don't need any complex, automated processes or tools to do it, either.

If you did that, you'd go from 7% supporting the church to 8%. That may seem like a small amount, but it's actually an increase in over 14%! Ten more families and you get a 14% increase in financial gifts and volunteers. That's huge! If you did that for seven years in a row (just ten families per year), you would double your funds and volunteers in seven years. How does that sound? Pretty nice I bet, and not all that difficult. That's the power of thinking big but working incrementally.

WHAT THE DEVIL WANTS

Here are some things the devil would love for you to do next:

- Try to do too much, get too ambitious, and believe that you have to save the world by yourself.
- Start complaining about all the things you just realized are being done wrong at your church.
- Get overwhelmed, lose your peace, and become discouraged.
- Start blaming others or what came before you.
- Compare yourself to others.
- Get distracted with the details or with making things too perfect.
- Decide to do something big . . . but put off starting until *tomorrow.*

Don't give the devil what he wants. Instead, pray, fast, and then turn every one of those things around on him.

When you want to complain about something, thank somebody instead. When you want to blame someone, encourage them. When you get too ambitious, be content with less. When you start to worry or get overwhelmed, decide to trust God more. And when you are tempted to put it off until tomorrow, do one small thing to move it forward today.

CHAPTER TWENTY-THREE

My Hope

"I have said this to you, so that in me you may have
peace. In the world you face persecution. But take
courage; I have conquered the world!"

—John 16:33

In the many years of doing this work, I've gotten to meet a lot of amazing, inspiring people. They are probably a lot like you—having found themselves (by God's providence) in a leadership role at their church, doing an often thankless job filled with frequent frustrations, tasked with doing too much with too little, and exhausted (sometimes jaded) by a never-ending struggle with a fallen world. And yet, by the grace of God, you soldier on with a peaceful joy, unwavering faith, and selfless love, all of which communicate far more than anything you'll learn from this book. That gives me great hope. You give me hope. And it is a great privilege to join you on this mission.

At Flocknote we are praying for your important work, where big things are at stake and souls hang in the balance. We are praying for the precious relationships that make evangelization even possible. We are praying as Jesus prayed: that we may all be one. And we are working tirelessly alongside you, going after that lost sheep and leading them to the treasure upon treasure that God wants to give them. If we work together, maybe one day *everyone* will know *what's keeping them in the Church*.

ONE LAST THING

"If I speak in the tongues of mortals and of angels,
but do not have love, I am a noisy gong
or a clanging cymbal."

—1 Corinthians 13:1

Remember, we can execute everything in this book perfectly, but if we don't have love, we'll still fail. The message will not get through. We can't lead people beyond this world by thinking according to the world. Rather, it requires operating with a logic that transcends it. It requires loving foolishly, "for God's foolishness is wiser than human wisdom" (1 Cor. 1:25).

Our work involves mysterious forces that we do not understand. It is work in which you bring five loaves and two fishes and thousands of people are fed. The math will never add up, as there is no counting angels, nor measuring grace. It goes beyond the business of metrics and on to miracles. Love and friendship are not about 80/20 rules, return-on-investment calculations, or meeting in the middle, but about going all the way. Love is not concerned with giving "enough" but only with whether I can give any more. It is lavish and generous beyond reason. If we want our message to get through, if we want people to know what's at stake and to realize the Great Story they're in, if we want them to follow, then our ministry must love like that.

It's Mary taking a year's-wages worth of ointment and "wasting" the whole thing on Jesus' feet (John 12). When you know who Jesus is, it is the most sensible and logical thing to do. But to the world (and to Judas), it makes no sense. Good! Let such "foolishness" shake a dulled and bored people. Let it roar with a sublime kind of love that wakes a sleeping world. Let it powerfully communicate the infinite joy right now being offered to everyone—that they might follow him.

What's Next?

Invite your staff and ministry leaders to read this book together. Discuss it as a team and start engaging your flock like never before. Get bulk copies at whytheyfollow.com.

Go deeper at whytheyfollow.com.

- How to tell the Great Story (Free Short Course)
- How to set goals that motivate (Free Short Course)
- Our podcast, *The Finding Uno Show* (findingUno.com)
- Flocknote blog (flocknote.com/blog)
- And more!

Try Flocknote for free. Lead your flock somewhere big and meaningful!

- Reach your flock when you need to (and hear back).
- Build a clean, up-to-date member database.

- Raise more money, from more people, faster than ever before!

Join Uno to go after the lost! Get a FREE Uno sticker. Stick him somewhere fun (your car, computer, favorite water bottle). Every time you see him, he'll remind you of our shared mission to go after the lost. Go to flocknote.com/uno to get your free Uno sticker!

Acknowledgments

Special thanks to the Flocknote team, whose joyful service and loving hearts inspire me every day. To the Flocknote Book Team, who were kind when I wrote poorly and whose brilliant contributions improved this book tremendously. To Betty and all the leaders of the Church who so lovingly tend their flocks, especially those that shared their beautiful stories here so that others may benefit. To my beautiful wife, my best friend and the best writer I know. To my children, my favorite characters in this Great Story.

Notes

CHAPTER ONE

Not only are Americans rapidly becoming less Christian, but we are doing so at an increasing rate: "In U.S., Decline of Christianity Continues at Rapid Pace," Pew Research Center, October 17, 2019, pewforum.org/2019/10/17 /in-u-s-decline-of-christianity-continues-at-rapid-pace/.

to give, to impart, or to transmit something in order that you might share it in common: Dictionary.com, s.v. "communicate," accessed September 29, 2022, dictionary.com/browse/communicate.

CHAPTER TWO

Gallup asked ten thousand people what they want from the leaders they choose to follow: "Successful Leadership: The 4 Needs of Followers," Gallup, March 9, 2021, gallup.com/cliftonstrengths/ en/334373/successful-leadership-4-needs-followers.aspx.

CHAPTER FOUR

"Christianity is a statement which, if false, is of no importance, and, if true, of infinite importance. . . .": C.S. Lewis, "Christian Apologetics," in *God in the Dock: Essays on Theology and Ethics*, ed. Walter Hooper (Grand Rapids, MI: Eerdmans, 2014), 102.

CHAPTER FIVE

all of human history is really his story: A paraphrase of Peter Kreeft. See, for example, *Food for the Soul: Reflections on the Mass Readings (Cycle C)* (Park Ridge, IL: Word on Fire, 2021), 3.

Christianity is first a way of seeing the whole of things: The University of Mary, *From Christendom to Apostolic Mission: Pastoral Strategies for an Apostolic Age* (Bismarck, ND: University of Mary, 2020).

"life is not primarily a quest for pleasure . . .": Harold S. Kushner, foreword to *Man's Search for Meaning*, by Viktor Frankl (Boston: Beacon, 2006), x.

"Meaning that is self-made is in the last analysis no meaning. . . .": Joseph Ratzinger, *Introduction to Christianity* (San Francisco: Ignatius, 2004), 73.

CHAPTER SIX

Sherry Weddell's brilliant book: Sherry A. Weddell, *Forming Intentional Disciples: The Path to Knowing and Following Jesus* (Huntington, IN: Our Sunday Visitor, 2012).

People buy into the leader before they buy into the vision: John Maxwell, "Teamwork and Vision Go Hand in Hand," Johnmaxwell.com, March 26, 2013, johnmaxwell.com/blog/teamwork-and-vision-go-hand-in-hand/.

"We do not really want a religion that is right where we are right. . . .": G.K. Chesterton, *The Catholic Church and Conversion* (New York: Macmillan, 1926), 95

"We do not want, as the newspapers say, a Church that will move with the world. . . .": G.K. Chesterton, *The New Witness* newspaper column, quoted in Maisie Ward, *Gilbert Keith Chesterton* (Lanham, MD: Rowman & Littlefield, 2006), 398.

CHAPTER SEVEN

"Shows much more of himself to some people than to others . . .": C.S. Lewis, *Mere Christianity* (New York: HarperCollins, 2001), 164.

"The ill-educated Christian turning gradually into the ill-tempered agnostic . . .": G.K. Chesterton, *The Everlasting Man* (New York: Dodd, Mead & Co., 1926), xiv.

CHAPTER EIGHT

A rapid decline in family stability: Gretchen Livingston, "About One-Third of U.S. Children Are Living with an Unmarried Parent," Pew Research Center, April 27, 2018, pewresearch.org/fact-tank/2018/04/27/about-one-third-of-u-s-children-are-living-with-an-unmarried-parent/.

Fewer close relationships: "Loneliness and the Workplace: 2020 U.S. Report," Cigna, January 2020, cigna.com/static/www-cigna-com/docs/about-us/newsroom/studies-and-reports/combatting-loneliness/cigna-2020-loneliness-report.pdf.

An increase in depression and anxiety: Dylan Walsh, "Study: Social Media Use Linked to Decline in Mental Health," MIT Sloan, September 14, 2022, mitsloan.mit.edu/ideas-made-to-matter/study-social-media-use-linked-to-decline-mental-health.

The average person spends 47.6 hours/week sleeping: Jeffrey Jones, "In U.S., 40% Get Less Than Recommended Amount of Sleep," Gallup, December 19, 2013, news.gallup.com/poll/166553/less-recommended-amount-sleep.aspx.

CHAPTER NINE

People begin struggling to manage more than about 150 relationships: Simon Sinek, *Leaders Eat Last* (London: Penguin, 2017).

CHAPTER ELEVEN

"What information consumes is rather obvious . . .": Herbert A. Simon, "Designing Organizations for an Information-Rich World," in Martin Greenberger, *Computers, Communication, and the Public Interest* (Baltimore, MD: Johns Hopkins Press, 1971), 41.

"Turn the soil of the heart and make it more receptive to the planting of the Gospel seed": Robert Barron, *The Pivotal Players: 12 Heroes Who Shaped the Church and Changed the World* (Park Ridge, IL: Word on Fire, 2020), 212.

"Laughter strengthens your immune system, boosts mood, diminishes pain, and protects you from the damaging effects of stress . . .": Lawrence Robinson, Melinda Smith, and Jeanne Segal, "Laughter Is the Best Medicine," HelpGuide, accessed August 29, 2022, helpguide.org/articles/mental-health/laughter-is-the-best-medicine.htm.

"Doors in the walls of the world": Peter Kreeft, *Doors in the Walls of the World* (San Francisco: Ignatius, 2018).

The intellect alone rarely moves people into action: John Henry Newman, *An Essay in Aid of a Grammar of Assent* (New York: Catholic Publication Society, 1870).

As Matthew Kelly notes: Matthew Kelly, *The Four Signs of a Dynamic Catholic* (New York: Beacon, 2012).

CHAPTER TWELVE

Consistent research done on established Catholic parishes: Lydia Saad, "Catholics' Church Attendance Resumes Downward Slide," Gallup, April 9, 2018, news.gallup.com/poll/232226/church-attendance-among-catholics-resumes-downward-slide.aspx.

CHAPTER THIRTEEN

"A person's name is to that person the sweetest and most important sound in any language": Dale Carnegie, *How to Win Friends and Influence People* (New York: Gallery Books, 2022), 85.

CHAPTER FOURTEEN

6% of your followers see a given Facebook post—unless you pay extra: Aristide Basque, "Facebook Reach in 2022: How Many People See Your Posts?" K6 Agency, September 3, 2022, k6agency.com/facebook-reach/.

97% of text messages are read within fifteen minutes of delivery: Andy Gilhooley, "SMS Marketing vs. Email Marketing: Who Wins the Battle for Effectiveness?" RedEye, May 4, 2021, redeye.com/resources/sms-marketing-vs-email-marketing-who-wins-the-battle-for-effectiveness/.

CHAPTER FIFTEEN

Nora Ephron's most profound writing lesson: Greg McKeown, *Essentialism: The Disciplined Pursuit of Less* (New York: Crown Business, 2014), 73–74.

CHAPTER SIXTEEN

Peter Shankman's surprising workday: Peter Shankman, "The Greatest Customer Service Story Ever Told, Starring Morton's Steakhouse," Peter Shankman, August 18, 2011, shankman.com/the-greatest-customer-service-story-ever-told-starring-mortons-steakhouse/.

CHAPTER SEVENTEEN

The POST Method: Charlene Li and Josh Bernoff, *Groundswell: Winning in a World Transformed by Social Technologies* (Boston: Harvard Business Review, 2008).

CHAPTER TWENTY-TWO

"Trust in the slow work of God. . . .": Pierre Teilhard de Chardin, quoted in *Hearts on Fire: Praying with Jesuits*, ed. Michael Harter (Chicago: Loyola, 2004), 102.

Fulton Sheen wasn't called "the great communicator" because he winged it: Robert Barron, *The Pivotal Players: 12 Heroes Who Shaped the Church and Changed the World* (Park Ridge, IL: Word on Fire, 2020), 205.